To HEAL and ....

To HEAL and Not to HURT

A fresh approach to safeguarding in Church

Rosie Harper and Alan Wilson

DARTON·LONGMAN+TODD

First published in 2019 by
Darton, Longman and Todd Ltd
1 Spencer Court
140 – 142 Wandsworth High Street
London SW18 4JJ

ISBN: 978-0-232-53394-1

A catalogue record for this book is available from the British Library

Phototypeset by Judy Linard
Printed and bound in Great Britain by Bell & Bain Ltd, Glasgow

Contents

Preface

At eleven o'clock on the eleventh day of the eleventh month of 1918 the guns fell silent. One hundred years later one of us stood with 350 people on a crisp autumn day in a Buckinghamshire village, by a newly restored memorial to 39 local people. Over a quarter of the village's population attended this and other events in church that day.

The other of us was in the Market Square in Aylesbury. It was teeming with people – families with buggies, bikers, wheelchairs, young people, parents and veterans, the great and the good, emergency and armed services, cadets, Scouts and Guides, pipe band, the lot. The crowds were so dense the parade could scarcely get through. All over the country vast numbers of people gathered in silence to keep faith with the dead, to stand in solidarity, to hope for peace and, of course, to remember.

After silence at the memorial, the Buckinghamshire villagers processed into church. One remembering morphed into another. 'Do this in remembrance of me.' As a human and as a Christian community it's what we do. We remember.

Nobody at either memorial was re-living their experience. The wartime generation has almost entirely gone. The village church held a special service that evening for those who had been recently bereaved. It was called *Remembering with Love,* and for an hour a large congregation, almost 200 people, deliberately stepped into a space of recollection. The love and the pain were still there, but with the passing of time memory had been distilled, so that people remembered without having to re-live.

One holocaust survivor has described her experience in graphic terms. What happened to her in Dachau was like a large rock thrown into a still pond. For a while, powerful waves swamped her life. After a few years the surface looked calm. The ripples had gone, but the rock was still at the bottom of the pond. Raising it again made new waves that felt overwhelming. Remembering, for her, meant re-living.

We have learnt there is no such thing as what used to be called a 'historic case'. The abuser may be long dead, but the pain lives on. We have also learnt that, without compassion for the person concerned, dragging up the stone from the bottom is re-abuse. The Church must learn how to take past disclosures seriously in the present. Until that happens it is impossible to find restoration and freedom from pain.

The Christian faith is rooted in Remembering. Knowing that he was about to be killed Jesus said, 'remember me' and gave his friends a way to do that which is repeated constantly in churches around the world. The Eucharist, at its best, can turn re-living into remembrance, a form of love and thankfulness. A Church with a Eucharistic heart should be a good, safe, and healing place to do all kinds of remembering.

Sadly this isn't always the case. We are only just beginning to uncover the extent of abuse that has happened. Increasing numbers of people, with extraordinary courage, are now telling their stories. The Church is trying to respond, in its own way. Considerable resource is being put into making it less likely that people will be abused in church in future.

It's the remembering part that hasn't gone well. For most people who make a disclosure, speaking out and telling the story involves re-living it, and that's where the Church's response usually makes things worse. This book is an attempt to change that. Survivors' painful memories need to be acknowledged and owned by the whole Church community, before they can become a resource and source of wisdom.

When someone courageously speaks out about their abuse, we need to embrace that story, painful though it is, and allow the truth to dawn. When things go tragically wrong, we all have to take responsibility and understand that 'their' story is really also 'our' story. Then we can share the pain and, perhaps, the healing. Disturbingly, the way the Church has behaved towards them after things went wrong has almost always made things worse, often in life-changing ways.

We have had to pick carefully through a linguistic minefield to work out how to refer to people who have been damaged by abuse. 'Victims' has the virtue of conveying the seriousness of what has happened, but with the danger of defining them. Some survivors prefer to be designated as victims because that makes plain that the suffering does not end.

Some prefer the straightforward term 'abusee'. This has some clinical accuracy, but very few people we have met refer to themselves in this way.

Unless a criminal conviction had been secured, the British Government's Independent Inquiry into Child Sex Abuse (IICSA) has referred to abusees as 'complainants'. Whilst technically correct, this seems to minimise the position of people who have been assaulted in ways that never came to court, including those whose perpetrators have died before justice was achieved for them in court.

Most people we have met refer to themselves as survivors. This seems to take seriously what has happened and also acknowledge the courage and resilience we have found in so many of the people we've met. It also points to future hope. In the end we have chosen this term more often than any other.

A more technical question arises about whether or not to capitalise the word 'church.' We have decided to capitalise when the reference is theological or institutional, but not when speaking of a local church or generic term like 'churchwarden'.

We are both clergy of the Church of England, and almost all the people we have talked with suffered abuse in a Church of England church or school. We do not intend in any way to imply things are better or worse within our Church. It does, however, have its own distinctive challenges in responding well to survivors, which we hope to address in a positive way. We hope our approach may also be useful beyond our own denomination.

We have encountered many professionals along our way, lawyers, insurers, academics, communications officers, and social workers. We believe they all have vital roles to play. That said the Church has the ultimate responsibility for how it behaves, and cares. It needs to embrace its distinctive calling to embody the love of Christ in the real world.

It is hard to know where to begin to thank the hundreds of people who have informed, inspired and helped us in our search for understanding and some way out of the present church crisis over safeguarding. Some of these are themselves survivors of abuse, and we acknowledge the cost to them of all they have given us.

A few have made been particularly generous with time and expertise, including friends, colleagues, lawyers, journalists, experts and academics. In random order:

Rupert Bursell, Lisa Oakley, Martyn Percy, Peter Hay, Josie Stein, Matt Ineson, Jo Kind, Jayne Ozanne, Jeremy Pemberton, Andrew Graystone, Lucy Berry, Guy Elsmore, Maurice Tomlinson, Ian Elliott, Graham (Smyth Victim 004), Richard Scorer, Andrew Foreshew-Cain, Linda Woodhead, Gilo, Stephen Parsons, Vicky Beeching, Martin

Sewell, Carrie Pemberton-Ford, Tom Perry, and many others.

We need to emphasise that errors of fact or judgment that remain are entirely our responsibility and not theirs.

We are grateful to David Moloney and his colleagues at DLT for their help and encouragement, and especially for having the courage to publish on such a painful and complicated subject.

We are also acutely conscious of how much, in every way, we owe Tim and Lucy, our spouses and families, especially their forbearance and support in this project.

The guns fell silent on the eleventh hour of the eleventh day of the eleventh month. The Church's embarrassment and bungling with abuse survivors suggests this could be some kind of eleventh hour for the Church of England. It may well be on the threshold of its own #metoo movement.

Emphatically, we do not want the Church to stop being the Church – rather to start being truthful and authentic. There are undoubtedly instances where the Church gets it right. We would love to hear from people for whom this has happened. Our pastoral encounters with many survivors have shown us that, as far as safeguarding goes, the Church needs more than cosmetic surgery. It needs a heart transplant.

The Bad Faithed movement (http://www.badfaithed. org) held an inaugural conference, 'Home Truths' in London in 2018 dealing with abuse in clergy families. The poet Lucy Berry wrote this hymn parody for it, which drew nods of recognition from many of the survivors who were present:

In Purple, Invisible
With profound apologies to Walter Chalmers Smith

In purple invisible, Church only wise,
remote, inaccessible hid from our eyes,
self-blessed and inglorious.
Lost and in doubt
we stand here before you, cast down and cast out.

You're wholly unhasting and silent as light.
We're *wanting*. You're *wasting* your chance to do right.
We wither and perish
as leaves on the tree.
You blossom and flourish, for naught changeth Thee.

In purple, invisible, Church only wise,
remote, inaccessible, hid from our eyes,
What help will you render?
Or will you decide
to cross, in your splendour, to the other side?

© Lucy Berry 2018

Nobody we have met wants things to be like this. We are convinced they don't have to be. Survivors are not a threat to the Church, but a resource. They are the experts. First and foremost we have tried to listen to and understand the experiences of survivors themselves. The courage, wisdom and insight of many has been our guide and inspiration for this project. There is much to learn together from all they have experienced of the institution we represent. We dedicate this book to them.

Introduction: A Bad Joke?

Once upon a time, a rich young man saw a TV programme about monks who had given up everything to follow Christ. As he watched he became sad and agitated about the gap between his life as a city trader and the simple way of life portrayed on the screen. Longing gripped him. 'I know,' he said, 'I must return to my Catholic roots.' Always a man to start at the top, he decided to go to Rome and discuss the matter with the Pope.

Next week he was in St Peter's Square. The Holy Father was passing among the crowds, offering prayers and blessings. The city trader stood there in his Armani suit, near an old nun in a wheelchair, a small girl with a bunch of flowers and a filthy old tramp. As he passed along, the Pope spoke to the nun and the little girl but, oh dear, walked right past the rich young man and made a beeline for the tramp, in whose filthy ear he had a close personal conversation.

Why had he been ignored? The man got onto Wikipedia straight away. It said that St Francis swapped clothes with a beggar and forsook his riches. 'Of course!' he thought. 'If I swap clothes with this filthy old beggar, then perhaps the Pope will want to talk to me.' 'Dear brother', he said to the tramp. 'Let me have your clothes and you can have my Armani suit and the keys to my Ferrari …'

Next week he was back in the Square when the Pope came along. He spoke to an old priest, and a wounded war veteran and then, oh joy! came over to the rich young man in his rags. The Pope leaned in close and personal and whispered in his ear, 'Look here, buster, I thought I told you last week to get lost!'

It's not much of a joke. Its significance is that it was told us by a survivor of abuse. It summed up his experience of the Church. He was angry and more than disappointed to have been ignored, lied to, then blocked by senior ecclesiastical figures.

What happened to him represents a major failure in Christian leadership. The Rule of Benedict (64) instructs the Abbot

> to order all things so that the strong may have something to inspire them and the weak nothing they need run from.

Bishops were the last people our friend expected to see using their power to protect their own position. The prayer used to consecrate a bishop in the Church of England led him to expect something very different:

> Give *him* humility,
> that *he* may use *his* authority to heal, not to hurt;
> to build up, not to destroy...

Healing is at the heart of Christianity. 'Healing' and 'Salvation' itself are closely related. In the Gospels, Jesus often says, 'Your faith has saved you' to people he has just healed physically. It involves restoring wholeness and community as well. Lepers, like haemorrhaging women, are cured physically, but also restored to their communities so that they belong again. Healing is far more than physical cure.

People have every right, then, to expect the Church to be a place of safety and healing. Local churches are very often exactly that. People find them to be communities in which everyone matters. They show a high level of care and when things go wrong people work hard to try and put them right. In this sense, the local church can be said to be the hope of the world.

Introduction: A Bad Joke?

If this were the whole story, we would all be in paradise. But, unfortunately, we are not there yet.

The present authors are pastors. Between us we have racked up almost seventy years of pastoral ministry in the Church of England. In recent years we have listened with increasing dismay to more than seventy people who have had seriously damaging experiences in Church. Most of them describe themselves as 'Survivors' and we have used this term for them.

There is a variety of terminology, however, in this area. The IICSA Inquiry, for example, has a more restricted definition or 'survivors'. People are 'complainants' unless their abusers have been convicted. Many of those we meet, like survivors of John Smyth/Iwerne abuse, were abused by people who evaded the courts. This does not detract from the significance of their experience or the Church's response to it. Our purpose is not to judge who has or has not been abused, but to resource a better response to them from the Church.

Our encounters have revealed the disturbing degree to which the Church, and especially its senior pastors, can fall short of its healing vocation. Many people have told us about experiences of being blocked, patronised, blamed or ignored. These compound the hurt they have suffered, in a way that amounts to reabuse. This harm is very rarely, if ever, intended. It is still experienced, and cannot be ignored. How can an institution committed to healing people end up harming them instead?

Most institutions react poorly to being shamed. As the failures of the church are exposed and held up to public scrutiny, the pressure to circle the wagons and do nothing or do wrong actually increases. The shame of the institution works its way out on others, causing more pain. This tends to create more victims, and emotions become entrenched and toxic.

This book is an attempt to understand why good church people end up doing bad things, when the Christian faith should be able to break the cycle of pain, shame and blame. The cross is the ultimate symbol of shame. It absorbs it in suffering, and in silence and peace it breaks the spiral of violence. It does away with any need for scapegoats, and so brings about truth and reconciliation.

All abuse is ultimately about power. It is particularly wrong when authority is abused in church. As well as instructing his followers to baptise and break bread, Jesus washed their feet and told them to follow his example. He inverts the usual pattern of power relationships.

Confronted by disciples scrapping about their pecking order he rebukes them, and their mothers:

> You know that the rulers of the Gentiles lord it over them, and their great ones are tyrants over them. It will not be so among you; but whoever wishes to be great among you must be your servant, and whoever wishes to be first among you must be your slave; just as the Son of Man came not to be served but to serve, and to give his life a ransom for many... (Matthew 20:25-58)

The mark of a healthy and authentically Christian community, then, is not large numbers, inspiring worship, or dogmatic orthodoxy, but the way in which power is exercised within it. This principle applies at every level. Senior leaders do not get out of its implications just because they are busy, think they are very important or feel overburdened with responsibility.

A Church that does not pay close attention to the way power is exercised among its people undermines its own mission:

I give you a new commandment, that you love one another. Just as I have loved you, you also should love one another. By this everyone will know that you are my disciples, if you have love for one another.' (John 13:34-5)

Gandhi is often quoted as having said 'the measure of a civilisation is how it treats its weakest members'. If this principle is true, how much more might we expect it to hold in church, which claims to be the first fruits of a new humanity in Christ?

A Church that treats those who are harmed within it appropriately will not only be doing the right thing by them, but will be truer to its core mission.

The kind of progress that is necessary is about far more than protocols, policies and professional practice. Safeguarding is rightly considered to be everybody's responsibility. Therefore it cannot be outsourced to social workers, lawyers or insurers.

It is often said that the real issues in safeguarding, whether in religion, sport, media, education or healthcare arise from culture. Institutions have corporate assumptions and routines that are bigger than the individuals who comprise them. Culture, we are told, eats strategy for breakfast. It is the culture that has to change.

In a memorable address, following revelations about Australian soldiers indulging in sexist behaviour, General David Morrison sought to engage the whole Australian army in tackling the cultural context in which this had happened:

If you become aware of any individual degrading another then show moral courage and take a stand against it...The standard you walk past is the standard you accept.

So why do good Christians walk by? In Chapter 2 below we explore some possible theological reasons for this. Humanly speaking, there is a culture of 'nice' in the Church of England. The comedy character Reggie Perrin used to say, 'You're not really nice until you know how nice it is to be nice.' People in churches don't like to get involved or pry into others' lives. Usually they want to believe the best of their fellow Christians. That is commendable, but when destructive attitudes and behaviours go unnoticed. They are soon normalised, and then the most vulnerable people are likely to be hurt rather than healed. Domestic violence, sexism, spiritual abuse and bullying take many forms, especially in a culture where most things are seldom measured, including the use of power. That said, 'Somebody else should do something about it' is never an adequate response.

We have tried to show how diverse and complex church culture can be by basing our constructive models and proposals for the future on personal experience in many different areas of church life, not just sexual abuse. Our purpose is to help people identify places where power is being misused as early and effectively as possible.

Until we are all fully involved and accept moral responsibility for the flourishing of everybody, especially the most vulnerable among us, church life will struggle to be more than a bad joke.

Fifteen Tales from the Crypt

Safeguarding is about real lives. Therefore we have chosen to ground what we have to say about it in stories we have written, drawn from real experience. All of them, taken together, illustrate different aspects of how going to church can be bad for people.

We understand that our stories may make distressing reading for anyone whose personal experience chimes in too closely with the characters we have drawn. Readers who experience any discomfort can skip this section without entirely losing the thread of our argument. To help, we have provided a cast of characters in Appendix 1 (p. 205ff.) that should help anyone who has not read the tales make better sense of the rest of what we have to say. This list may also help relate the names we use later to their particular context.

We may also have, unwittingly, used trigger words that touch raw nerves. Even the names we have made up for our characters belong to real people out there. Should something from here play on any reader's mind, it would be wise to speak to someone like:

Minister and Clergy Sexual Abuse Survivors (MACSAS) 08088 010340 (www.macsas.org.uk)

Victim Support 0808 1689111 (www.victimsupport.org.uk)

Or the police, your doctor, a local Sexual Assault Referral Centre ... or your Diocesan Safeguarding Advisor.

It is often said that 'culture eats strategy for breakfast'.

The Church can only deal with abuse by changing its culture. Our stories identify a broad range of abusive behaviours and attitudes. These include child sex abuse but recognise that power is mishandled in the Church in many different ways. The experiences of spiritually abused young people, bullied ordinands and vicars, narcissistic clergy and victims of domestic violence need to be understood as symptoms of a broader Church culture in which power is used to harm people.

Some of the significant harm people we know have experienced in church is dramatic and some could be thought to be too low-key to matter. Some involves criminal behaviour. Much involves subtle forms of emotional and spiritual abuse. Some experiences have been widely reported and others have not and, perhaps, should not be. It is important that all testimonies are heard and can be talked about openly, including those that need to remain anonymous. We have fictionalised so as to be able to describe a wide range of experience, not just those cases in the public domain.

Survivor testimonies are full of sensitive details. Stories have to be real enough to shed light on some very sensitive and painful matters. We need to tell them in a way that respects personal dignity.

Churches are communities where confidentiality is often compromised, sometimes with the best of intentions, like rustling up community prayer or pastoral support. For survivors, however, broken confidence is usually experienced as re-abuse.

To make it possible to explore the human impact of abuse whilst respecting confidentiality we have remixed many of the things we have been told into 15 fictional miniatures. These speak of incidents that are by no means the most extreme we have encountered. We have chosen to pitch our scenarios in the middle ground so as not to make any survivor we know identifiable.

Many in the Church may have had experiences that resonate with ours. Our tales are fiction, but we can guarantee that everything of substance our characters say is based on genuine personal accounts.

That said, we need to underline a caveat from the movies:

> The stories, all names, characters, and incidents portrayed in this production are fictitious. No identification with actual persons (living or deceased), places, buildings, and products is intended or should be inferred.

It is important to underline that most of what happens in church is far from abusive. Usually in a healthy church everybody is somebody. People relate to others with warmth and respect. At their best churches are societies of friends who find meaning, delight and challenge in each other's company.

That's the good story. Millions of people find it in Church of England churches all the time. So why spoil things by telling negative stories? Why not simply look on the bright side of life?

Tales from the crypt are painful. They are hard to tell and to hear. But for the sake of survivors, and the Church's own wellbeing, it must listen to them, and act appropriately. The problem is not things going well, but what happens when they don't. A food company may make tasty meals with many satisfied customers. Should one of the company's products poison anybody, it has to put itself out to understand exactly what has happened and why. Only by doing that can it address the situation and put things right. Turning a blind eye is not an option:

> 'Religions that cannot admit and work to correct their lethal errors and flawed heroes do not deserve to survive. (Daniel C. Maguire, quoted in Elaine Storkey, *Scars Across Humanity:*

Understanding and Overcoming Violence Against Women, 2015, p. 187)

Cultures of complacency and denial come easily to large institutions. As one memorable book puts it *'Mistakes were made but not by me'*. To avoid this phenomenon, it is necessary for the Church to pay close attention when things go wrong. Negative experiences become vital opportunities to learn and change for good.

Here are 15 fictionalised miniatures, describing damaging experiences in church. We have tried to draw our characters compassionately, including the perpetrators. It is not unusual for an abuser to have been a victim themselves. People have their own internal reasons for behaving badly. These need to be understood without excusing anything.

Although they are fictitious the situations in which our characters find themselves may well draw wry smiles of recognition from many people who know church life from the inside. We will draw on them later to give substance to the non-fictional part of this book.

1. Mark

Mark was christened at St Agatha's by Father Archie, who seemed to have been there since the year dot. The vicar was a well-known character in his inner city parish. People remembered him during the war in his cassock doing his rounds and saying, 'Hitler's not going to stop me doing my job.'

Mark's parents had married late, and he was an only child. They seemed older than his friends' parents. Pauline, his mother, had felt apprehensive as she wheeled Mark in his buggy up to the vicarage door, but Father Archie had sat her down with a cup of tea and she knew from that moment that she was going to try going to church more.

At the christening, the vicar said, 'It won't be long before we've got a new boat boy!'

Pauline was really proud the day Mark first appeared in his scarlet cassock and tiny cotta. Stanley, the MC, had trained more boys than he'd had hot dinners.

Father Archie had been the vicar since well before retirement ages came in for clergy. 'They'll carry me out of that place one day,' he said. They did. He made some noises about retiring at 80, but smoking and gin caught up with him the year before in the form of heart failure.

The new vicar was Father Ian. Inevitably he seemed to be something of a new broom. Some didn't like him, but Pauline said, 'You've got to give him a chance.'

Mark had now moved up in the sanctuary and was really happy serving in church. After some initial jitters, Father Ian got into his stride and the small congregation actually seemed to be growing for the first time in years.

Mark was one of the few who managed to stick with church through his teenage years. He was a shy boy, but he managed his Duke of Edinburgh's Award, and by 19 was a Queen's Scout.

He met Anita through scouting. She wasn't as much a pillar of St Agatha's as Mark, but was happy that he was. They married young at 24, but Mark found physical intimacy was beyond him. Anita saw a poster at the doctors' surgery for Relate. 'We'll go together,' she said.

The night before their first meeting Mark and Anita talked properly about sex for the first time. As they talked about themselves, he became progressively more distressed and broke down.

'Father Ian ruined my life,' he said.

'What do you mean?' she asked. That's when everything came tumbling out.

'Why didn't you tell anyone?'

'I did try,' he said. 'I told Mum what Father Ian made

me do, but she told me off for making things up.'

'Well, you've got to tell someone now,' said Anita. 'Quite apart from what happened to you, he could still be a danger to other kids.'

By next morning, Mark knew Anita was right.

All he'd wanted was to forget what happened with Father Ian, but telling Anita had opened everything up again and it felt raw. He had to speak to someone. Perhaps that would help him put it all behind him.

Five years ago, Father Ian had become an archdeacon in another diocese. Mark and the scouts had put on much of his leaving do. He was secretly sickened by the nice things everybody else was saying about the vicar.

He wasn't comfortable about telling the secular counsellor at Relate, so he skirted round the subject with her. The following Sunday he went up to Father Robert after Mass and arranged a time to see him privately at the vicarage.

Mark knew and liked his parish priest. He loved being head server, but it wasn't easy to talk about this. Being in the vicarage brought back memories. He realised he wasn't as comfortable as he thought he should be, back again where it had all happened.

Father Robert was a good listener. He was deeply shocked by what he heard and promised he would seek advice from the bishop. He prayed with Mark, and there was real concern in his voice as he asked whether there was anything else the Church could do to help.

Father Robert was at Diocesan Synod Standing Committee the next week with Bishop Simon. They had a word together afterwards about the possibility of a curate next year. As they walked to their cars Father Robert said, 'By the way, I meant to tell you, my head server came to see me last week and he says he was molested a few years ago by my predecessor.'

'What?' said Bishop Simon. 'You mean Ian Montgomery? Do you think there's anything to it?'

'Mark's an excellent server, and everybody likes the lad. I don't think he's got it in him to lie,' said Father Robert.

Bishop Simon looked shocked. 'His dad was my tutor at St Vincent's. I reckon I'm only standing here today because of Father Montgomery. Great Man. Turns out he put in a bit of a word for me when this diocese fell vacant. Mandy's my god-daughter. It's not good. I know. Why don't I have a word with Bishop Kenneth? This is very sensitive. Leave it with me, Robert. I know I can trust you. Careless talk costs lives, you know!'

Four weeks later, at House of Bishops, Bishop Simon collared Bishop Kenneth at a coffee break.

'Bad news, I'm afraid, about your archdeacon Ian Montgomery. New vicar of his old parish says there's somebody – choirboy or server or something – claiming things happened in the vestry a few years ago.'

'Ian? No! He's good. Gets things done. Capable mission-minded Catholic. We've got precious few of them around these days. He's on the preferment list. Poor Ian. What are we going to do?'

'Why don't you check there's nothing in it, your end. An interview with coffee should do it. I'll check with my diocesan secretary and registrar and that should do the trick. If the choirboy wants counselling, I'm sure something local can be arranged. The vicar can deal with all that.'

Three weeks later, Bishop Kenneth approached Archdeacon Ian after Senior Staff.

'We need to have a private word, I'm afraid, Ian. Trouble at the mill. There's a choirboy at your old place going around saying things were going on in the vestry involving you.'

'The choir? No. I never had anything to do with them.

Mrs Bartlett ruled the choir with a rod of iron. That might be actionable. Nothing to do with me.'

That evening Bishop Kenneth phoned Bishop Simon.

'I've had a word with my Archdeacon. Nothing in it. He's given me his personal assurances he never went anywhere near the choir. The choir mistress was a famous old dragon. The boy must be troubled in some way....'

The night after the next House of Bishops, Bishop Simon phoned Anthony his registrar. 'Tony, just a passing cloud, I think, but it could blow up in our faces. Robert Gregory's got a choirboy saying there were goings on in the vestry at St Agatha's a few years ago. What do I do?'

'Who knows about it? I'd get straight onto Lucinda at comms and get a statement behind your ear in case anything gets out. Legally, you have to stay out of this one. If there's a CDM Kenneth will deal with it but you could have to give evidence. You did something about it. That's what matters.'

With some relief, Bishop Simon said, 'Okay. We'll get a statement together. My diocesan secretary can check out any liability issues. I'll let you know if anything else happens this end.'

He picked up the phone again, this time to his Archdeacon.

'You won't know anything about this, Steve, but there's been a flap at St Agatha's. Robert says he's got a choirboy who says things went on in the vestry years ago. I've had a word with Bishop Kenneth, who's interviewed Ian. He's had personal assurances from Ian that there's nothing to it. I'm getting Lucinda to draft us a statement in case the boy goes to the press. Robert can deal with the pastoral side.'

'Oh heck,' said Archdeacon Steve. 'The lad could be really messed up. We could rustle up five hundred for counselling if that helps. I'll check with Robert. I'm seeing him at the clergy conference.'

Next month at the diocesan clergy conference, Archdeacon

Steve had a coffee with Father Robert. 'Bishop Simon's told me all about your predecessor's spot of bother in the vestry. Bishop Kenneth has checked carefully with Archdeacon Ian, and there's nothing to it. The boy must be making it up. There is a counselling fund, if that helps sort him out.'

'No need for that, I suspect,' said Father Robert. 'Mark's got a spiritual director, of course, and this sounds like one for him. I'll have a word.'

Ten years passed.

Mark and Anita had worked hard at their marriage, but they didn't make it. They divorced by mutual agreement after two years, with no children involved. They remained friends, but their friendship faded somewhat after two years when Anita married again. A year or so later she moved to Sussex and soon enough had two children.

Mark got his head down at work and in his church and scouting life, but felt life was very empty. Mark's confidence, undermined by abuse, drained away as the years passed. The ripples ceased on the surface, but the stone at the bottom of the pond was always there.

Bishop Simon and Bishop Kenneth had retired.

One Friday the *Church Times* dropped through Mark's letterbox. 'New Bishop of Axminster' said the headline. 'The Venerable Ian Montgomery. Archdeacon of Bardwell ....'

Mark was devastated. Rage welled up in him. He kicked the wall and shouted. 'Bloody hell! Father Ian? The bastards! They couldn't! How can they do this to me? This time I'm going to the papers!'

He knew Gemma, a reporter on the local paper. She had helped with Scouting events in the past. She came round to see him that evening.

Dioceses all had Safeguarding Advisors now, and Sheila had recently been appointed by Bishop Simon's old diocese. The following week, she phoned Bishop Christopher urgently.

'Bishop, a local journalist has been onto Lucinda for a statement about a man called Ian Montgomery. Someone at St Agatha's is alleging abuse, years ago. The priest was a man called Ian Montgomery We need to check his blue file and get something out sharpish.'

'Oh no!' said Bishop Christopher. 'Ian Montgomery? *The* Ian Montgomery? He was in the *Church Times* last week. He's an archdeacon up North somewhere. He's becoming a bishop. Just got Axminster. The file's probably gone to Lambeth. This could take ages. I'll get Lucinda to draft us something. It'll be a tricky one, though. We haven't got anything here any more.'

Next month Gemma had written up Mark's story. 'Sex in the Vestry –Vicar and Altar Boy.'

Lucinda duly put out her appropriate statement: 'The Church takes safeguarding very seriously especially the welfare of victims. The case may give rise to a criminal investigation, so it would be inappropriate to comment further.'

The story was a major item at next Senior Staff.

'How are we going to handle this?' asked Bishop Christopher. 'If a reporter came round and poked a microphone at me, could I just feign surprise and say I didn't know anything about Montgomery? Before my time? That sort of thing?'

Archdeacon Steve spoke up. 'I remember this one came up ten years ago. We dealt with it fully at the time. There was a rigorous inquiry in the other diocese, and they decided the choirboy was probably making it up. Robert Jackson was the vicar. He handled the pastoral side. We offered the lad counselling.'

Lucinda spoke next. 'We've got our statement out. The nationals haven't picked it up, thank God. Today's story is tomorrow's fish and chip paper. I would leave it at that unless something else happens.'

'I checked with Lambeth,' said Bishop Christopher. 'There

wasn't anything in the file. But it says on the back the file was weeded in 2006. Was that Data Protection? That wouldn't look good if we ever got an inquiry. Lambeth contacted Bishop Kenneth and he says safeguarding was the bane of his life. He had a few of these, but he can't remember this particular one. If anything happened, it wasn't in his diocese, anyway.'

'What about the past cases review in 2009?' asked Bishop Christopher.

'Nothing,' said Patrick, the diocesan secretary. 'We found 127 files, so Lambeth revised the criteria down, and we managed to trim them to 32. In the end they only reported two from us. I don't know how that happened. We'd certainly have noticed if Ian Montgomery made the shortlist, let alone the final cut. Anyway, technically it wasn't our diocese anyway.'

Patrick was anxious, though, about liability. Would Insurance cover it? He'd find out. 'Do we need to get Safeguarding in here with us? Sheila?'

'I've had a word with her,' said Bishop Christopher. 'She doesn't know anything about it. Way before her time. If anything else happens, I will, of course, brief her.'

Desmond had been the Cathedral Dean for over twenty years.

'We really don't need to make a drama out of a crisis,' he said. 'We've had a few of these down the years and they always blow over. The kid or his parents kick up, but it never goes anywhere. The best way to deal with these people is ignore them. They always go away in the end.'

2. Anna

Anna was 16. She was not brought up as a Christian, but her friend Suzy sang in the local church choir and was always on about her friends and things that happened at church. Suzy encouraged Anna to come along to choir practice, and although she didn't think she was particularly musical, she joined the choir. Soon she was in church most weeks.

One Sunday the vicar announced there would be a confirmation service in a few months' time and invited anyone interested to sign up for classes. 'Shall we?' said Suzy. 'Vince the curate is running them, and he'll make it fun. We don't have to get confirmed if we don't fancy it.' 'Let's,' replied Anna. 'I don't know if I fancy confirmation, but I might just get to fancy Vince!'

Every Friday evening a small group met in the choir vestry. Vince told funny stories. He made everything come alive for Anna. He took what she had to say seriously. She loved that, and when he asked her to do a reading at the confirmation service, she felt really special. It was a shame the classes were finishing, and she was delighted when Vince invited her round to talk about whether it was time to start a youth group at St Michael's.

That first week she stayed till ten, and Vince gave her a lift home. 'Let's meet again next week' he said. 'Talking to you means a lot to me and there's so much we could do.' 'Shall I come with Suzy?' Anna asked. 'I don't think so,' said Vince. 'Too many cooks ....'

Anna thought about their next meeting all week. She was bowled over on Wednesday to get a friend request from Vince on Facebook. On Thursday, she actually got a text from him – 'Can't wait for tomorrow.'

Six months later, during netball practice, Anna felt sharp stomach pains. An ambulance was called, and she found herself in A&E. 'Anna,' said the nurse, 'have you missed any periods recently? We've run some routine tests. Do you realise you're pregnant?'

She felt desolate and utterly alone. There was nobody else, only Vince. She hadn't gone on the pill because she was afraid her parents would find out. Vince had told her not to worry. Being together was God's will so she wouldn't get pregnant.

3. Jenny

Jenny grew up in a strong loving Christian family. When she was 14 everything about Jesus fell into place for her, and she committed herself to Christ. She joined the Christian Union at University. When she moved to a town in the West Country for her first job, she looked for a church where she could feel at home.

She was delighted to find a proper church – Holy Trinity. People called it HT. Mike the vicar was a dynamic leader, well known for his inspiring teaching. She made good friendships, and soon came to enjoy being part of the church family very much.

About a year later, HT had a rethink on admin and advertised for a Vicar's PA. Jenny prayed about it and felt strongly called to apply, even though she hadn't yet got a secretarial qualification as such. She discussed her sense of calling with her house group. They prayed about it together, and this boosted her confidence to go ahead and apply.

She was delighted when she got the job.

Three people worked in the church office, and there were often volunteers and members of the public of one sort or another around. Mike would walk through to his own office at the back in a friendly cheerful way. He saw himself as very much a people person – always there for everybody. He was often quite tactile.

One day Jenny went into work with a migraine. She felt she should probably have stayed at home, but didn't want to let the others down. Work was far more than a secular job – a real vocation.

She told Mike she was not feeling 100 per cent. He had a powerful healing ministry and she was delighted when he offered to pray with her. She found the experience rather smothering, up close and personal. Afterwards he gave her a big long hug to reassure her God loved her.

31

That was the first time she felt at all uncomfortable with Mike, but she blamed herself for that.

When Mike was out at lunch, Fiona the receptionist said, 'That was a long time with Mike! Are you okay?'

'What do you mean okay? He's rather tactile, isn't he? I didn't feel that good about it, but I guess that's just Mike,' Jenny replied.

'Actually,' Fiona said, 'we've learnt to keep an eye out for each other when Mike's about. A few years ago, he was rather touchy feely with one of us, and she complained to the churchwardens. They had to have words with Mike about it.'

Three months later Jenny came into work in tears. Her cat, Socks, had been run over, and she was distraught.

Fiona made her a cup of tea, and when Mike came into work, he was very sympathetic. They talked and prayed together, and, again, Mike gave her a big long hug afterwards. Now she felt distinctly uncomfortable especially when, to her horror, she realised he was sexually aroused.

She phoned her mum, who said, 'You need to get another job!' Jenny was now in turmoil. God had called her to work for Mike in the church office. It was a vocation not a job. Maybe she was just being oversensitive.

Anyway, if she said anything, would she ever be believed, or would people blame her for leading him on?

4. Peter

Peter is one of London's rising young barristers. He doesn't go to church any more except for family occasions, but when he was at boarding school, he had been involved with an Evangelical youth camp. It was targeted at boys from leading public schools. If tomorrow's leaders could be won for Christ, the nation would be transformed.

Peter was not one of the camp's success stories.

When he went up to Oxford he tried to get involved

in the Christian Union, but sport and a girlfriend who was distinctly cool about Christian things took their toll.

By the time he left, he occasionally went to college chapel, but not Christian Union. Marriage and two daughters added family responsibilities to the demands of study, then a rising career in commercial law. He seemed destined for the top, anyway.

Around his thirty-fifth birthday he was picking up the day's news after the children had gone to bed. Suddenly he recognised the face of someone he had been at school with. He turned up the sound. Jolyon was describing in vivid terms life at the Christian camp they had both attended years before. The leader had been sentenced that day to eight years for child sex offences. The story brought memories flooding back.

Peter felt sick. He had suspected at the time something was going on involving Jolyon and others. He had not known what to do about it then, and as faith faded, he had shut off the whole world of camp.

Next day his office phone rang. It was a Tania, a journalist from the BBC. Jolyon had given her Peter's name, saying that as his former camp officer he must have known something was going on. What light could he throw on the camps, for Jolyon's sake if not for his own? It seemed that other boys had been involved and were seeking justice after many years.

Peter didn't really want to have anything to do with the matter, but the reporter was insistent it would help Jolyon. Perhaps she was right. It could help others. There was no getting away from the stories about the camps. They were all over the media. He felt bad about having said and done nothing all those years before. If he simply blocked her it might even look as though he had something to hide.

He cleared the diary for a couple of hours next day, and Tania came to see him. Strictly off the record he shared his doubts and memories of all sorts of goings on that had raised his suspicions. Just talking about it brought it all back.

A few boys had seemed especially close to the leader, a kind of personal posse. Rumour had it they had special Bible studies and times of prayer with him. One or two had disappeared suddenly from camp, and stories had circulated in the dorms. The real elite, seven hand-picked dormitory officers, were taken on special camping trips to Wales, where all kinds of off-piste activities were said to have gone on.

Tania was most grateful. He had given her two new names to follow up, and nobody else had told her as much about the Leader's posse. Could she interview him on camera?

'Of course not,' he snapped. 'Can't you see this is private? It's my friends you're talking about. If it ever got out that I had spoken to the media, they would come after me. That would be the end of my career...'

5. Karen

Karen and David met at University, where they both read English. Initially, David was very much more committed to his faith than Karen, although she was very happy to string along with his Christian activities. They had a CU Bible Study in their digs. That's where she got to know students like her who took the Bible seriously, not like Sunday School. They had real faith. After a few months, she gave her life to Jesus. Being a committed Christian became the centre of her life and sharing it with David made it all the more special.

Both became teachers, but the day they married her mum said to her, 'You'll end up as a vicar's wife, you know!' She just laughed it off at the time, but ....

She prayed every day for her sister Jackie to become a Christian. She was so near but yet so far.

'I don't mind Jesus, Karen, but I just don't think I could ever be the little woman like you are with David. You actually do obey him. I couldn't ever do that for a man, however much I loved him!'

Ten years on, David was the Rector of St Nat's. Life was very full on, with 350 people on a Sunday and a large student ministry. Karen gave up teaching after Asher, their fourth child arrived. Her hands were full, but she still helped lead a life group, and supported David in every way she could. She was protective of him. Lord knows he needed it sometimes, and she felt a secret glow of pride when she overheard people calling St Nat's 'David Hamilton's church'.

Thursday was always a taxing day. Everyone seemed to have something on and needed a lift to it and picking up afterwards. Rebekah had dancing. Reuben went to Impact (the St Nat's youth ministry). Asher had Little Fishes. Friday was David's day off, but Karen was often too tired to care.

That Thursday, Leadership Team hadn't gone well for David. His women's minister, Emma, was usually very good in team meetings, but that day she had argued, and David felt she was getting at him. Karen had got the children off to bed, loaded the dishwasher, and was ready to fall into bed herself.

She was already asleep by the time David came up from his study and joined her. As he climbed into bed, she turned over with her back to him.

David felt angry and rejected. First Emma. Now his own wife.

'Come on, Karen, I've had a hell of day!'

She turned her back more deliberately.

Then something snapped for David. Roughly, he grabbed her shoulders and pushed himself down on her ....

Next day both were sullen.

'David we've got to talk about last night. You frightened me.'

'Really? But you're my wife. There's nothing to talk about. If you just learnt to behave like my wife, we'd be fine.'

'What?' said Karen.

'No, seriously,' said David, trying hard to calm down. 'You know what the Scriptures say. "Wives do not deny your husbands." 1 Corinthians 7:5. It's perfectly simple, woman! "Wives obey your husbands like you do the Lord." Win me. Don't criticise me all the time and then let me down when I need you.'

'But, David,' said Karen, 'I know that. I really try. I do love you but it's not easy. I don't think you know how much you hurt me sometimes.'

'You seem to think you're the only person in the world who gets hurt. Christians always have to suffer. Jesus said we would. It's part of the deal. 1 Peter 1:6, "now for a little while you may have to suffer grief in all kinds of trials ...".'

The next week, Jackie came around for coffee.

'Are you okay, Karen?'

'Not really. Asher's nursery teacher collared me after school today. She says he wet himself. He got really upset. When he lost it, he said "Please don't tell Daddy! He gets very cross with me when he's angry".'

'And does he?' asked Jackie.

'Not really,' said Karen. 'I think Miss Ridsdale's over-reacting. She isn't a Christian, you see. She doesn't get it. We've got a biblical marriage. Of course we discipline the children. Of course David needs to be firm sometimes, even with me. Why would she understand? They've got all these secular policies at school, so of course they don't see. It's different for Christians ....'

The next summer was David and Karen's 20th Wedding anniversary. David was out when Angela, the churchwarden, popped round with a houseplant as a present.

'You're so lucky, Karen,' said Angela. 'I don't know how you and David do it! It can't be easy when he's working so hard. But I'm sure he couldn't manage it without the woman behind the man!'

Karen went quiet.

'And four lovely children, all walking with the Lord! You're so lucky! Actually, it's not lucky is it. It's marrying the man God planned for you and sticking together through thick and thin. We're so blessed to have a minister who's a real role model for the rest of us!'

Karen began to sob.

Then it all came tumbling out. When she gingerly pulled up her sleeves Angela could see angry bruises.

Angela walked slowly back with a very heavy heart.

You can never tell what goes on behind closed doors. But David? Really? And why had she promised she wouldn't tell a soul?

Every time she saw Karen wearing long sleeves now, she knew the reason why.

6. Malcolm

PCC meetings were Malcolm's least favourite bit of the job. In his curacy they'd been okay. There were only four a year, chaired by the vicar. Now, in his first parish, there was a meeting every month except August, with Standing Committee the week before – twenty-two evenings he dreaded.

On 15 July it was the last PCC before the summer holidays. People were tired and ready for a break. The main item was Harriet's proposal to start a Thursday drop-in for carers. She'd done her homework with plans and costings, as well as a list of volunteers from the congregation. The main bone of contention was the line in the business plan about buying a modern wall-mounted water heater to replace the old stainless steel urn that everybody knew was on its last legs.

'In the whole scheme of things,' Harriet said, '£500 isn't the National Debt. Anyway, it would pay back through increased donations at the drop-in. That way we could upgrade our kitchen. It would be better for everything we do in church.'

'My dear girl,' said Barry the Treasurer, 'I think you've got a bit ahead of yourself here. You're not the first person to come up with this idea, and you won't be the last. I've always found when you really go into it, there's no need. Once you get one of those things in a church people start using it all the time. You'll find our electric bill goes through the roof. You ladies love your gadgets, I know. My Eileen was just the same. Anyway, we're not made of money. What women forget is you can only spend it when you've got it. Someone has to earn it first!'

Malcolm watched Harriet's face redden. He felt he ought to say something to support her, but he knew he wouldn't. Like everyone else in the room he was secretly scared of Barry. Anything anyone suggested got the same treatment.

In some ways it was understandable.

He remembered visiting Barry when Eileen died last year. Barry had told a very sad story. He'd been a skilled engineer for thirty years and then the company had been taken over. Production moved to Malaysia, and there were no more engineering jobs at Nettleship's. Barry had got a part-time job as a school handyman, but it wasn't the same.

But at least he had his church. When Barry took over as treasurer, he felt what it was like to be respected again. There was lots of sorting out to do. Nobody knew where the money came from or where it went, and Barry had been on a largely successful mission to sort that out. He was proud of running a tight ship, with everything signed for properly in his own neat squiggle.

Trouble was, Malcolm felt, Barry was becoming a liability. People were afraid to work with him, even speak with him. His pedantic way of shooting down anyone and everyone in flames was killing off all initiative.

Malcolm came home from holiday that August and picked up the phone to Noreen, the PCC secretary. 'I'm sorry, Malcolm, didn't anyone tell you? Barry gave me my cards while you were away. He said I hadn't done the statistics for mission form properly, and this wasn't the first time, so he'd do it from now on.'

Malcolm knew he had to do something now. As soon as he was off the phone to Noreen, he called Barry. 'Oh yes, Malcolm, I had to do it. If you want a job done properly you have to do it yourself!'

Malcolm put down the phone and wept. Any proper vicar would be able to handle someone like Barry.

7. Geoff

Geoff was raised as a Christian, and, as far back as he could remember, he had always wanted to join the Police. He left school at 16, and for two years worked in a bike shop, itching for the day he would be old enough to start at Hendon. He was proud to attest that he would

> well and truly serve the Queen in the office of constable, with fairness, integrity, diligence and impartiality, upholding fundamental human rights and according equal respect to all people ....

That fitted in well with his faith.

Geoff's career in the police led through sergeant's exams, which he passed early, to the rank of inspector. He was now married with two children, and the usual pressures of the job were bearing down on his family and his faith.

Maybe God wanted something else for him.

He went to see his vicar and within two years had been selected and was on a training scheme for ordained ministry. It was a tough stretch keeping his day job going along with all the study, but Prue, his wife, was solidly behind him, and he managed.

So it was that on his 39th birthday he found himself outside the Cathedral with a small crowd of ordinands in his new robes and collar, nervous but more than ready to go.

His training incumbent was Sally. She knew the ropes in church. Her father and grandfather had been clergy. Grandfather had actually been an archdeacon. She hugged him at the Peace, and he felt real confidence about what lay ahead.

Geoff's first staff meeting two days later was at the Vicarage, two miles away. He went on his bike and, would you believe it, he had a puncture. He'd dealt with enough of those back in the bike shop, but it made him five minutes late.

'Geoff,' said Sally, 'let me make this clear. This is not a hobby. You wouldn't want a priest to show up late for your mum's funeral, would you?'

Geoff wanted to defend himself but thought better of it. Best start off on a friendly footing. 'Sorry, Sally,' he said. 'It won't happen again.'

'I hope not,' she replied.

One thing Geoff had learnt in the police was teamwork. You cover for your colleagues, and sometimes you have to carry the can for them. When Mrs Bridges' purse was stolen from the vestry during choir practice, Sally blamed him for leaving the door unlocked. He knew he hadn't been at Choir Practice that week, but she didn't want to know.

Remembrance Sunday came around the following year, with a shorter Parish Communion in church followed by two minutes' silence at the war memorial.

As far as Geoff knew he'd done a good job. Hundreds came, the timings were right, and the British Legion seemed delighted. Sally gave the blessing followed by some notices. 'I'm sure we all forgive the Curate this once for wearing a poppy on his chasuble. It's a classic Curate mistake. He's a bit of an Ecclesiastical Wally, but he'll learn!'

Geoff felt humiliated but knew he couldn't show it. He felt 16 all over again, being told off in the bike shop in front of a customer.

Christmas Eve was always busy, and everyone was tired. At the crib service Geoff had told the story for the children. Eyes glistened, parents beamed, and on the way out people said what a lovely service it had been. Really Christmassy.

Getting ready for the midnight service, Sally cornered him in the vestry.

'Honestly, Geoff, you're hopeless. You've ruined Christmas for the servers. Sean is really upset. He says some idiot put the Bambino in the Crib before midnight. Can you go and get it back? I'll make peace with the servers for you.'

'I'm sorry, Sally. I had no idea.'

'Well that's your trouble, isn't it, Geoff. You've got no idea. Usual old thing. Story of your life.'

As he went out to the crib, he realised all the microphones were on. Everybody had heard ….

8. Jason

Linda, churchwarden at St Barnabas, knew she had to tell the archdeacon.

'I'm really sorry to have to phone you about something like this, Chris,' she said, 'but at the last visitation you said you wanted churchwardens to come to you with their concerns. Truth is things really aren't working out with Jason. If it was just me, I'd grin and bear it, but I've had a dozen people come to see me in the last couple of weeks.'

'Funny you should say that,' said Chris, 'I've had a few letters myself about Jason – Pippa your ordinand and a woman called Mrs Murdoch from the Co-op Funeral Service.'

'I know,' said Linda. 'Pippa told us last week she's going to go forward with ordination, but with Harry at St Peter's. We were shocked. She grew up here, and we think of her as very much one of our own.'

The following week Linda and the Archdeacon met.

'We were really excited when Jason was appointed two years ago,' she said. 'We knew he'd make a few changes. That's not the problem, though. In some ways your letter from the Co-op says it all.

'"He smelt of drink at the funeral." Same thing with us on Ash Wednesday. Mrs Smith in the choir had to help him get into his robes. When I asked whether he wanted someone else to take the service he just laughed and said, "Why can't I have a drink on a hot day if I want without some silly bitch complaining?"

'"He was rude and aggressive to the sexton at the crematorium." We've certainly experienced that.'

'"There was an inappropriate dirty joke in his address..." Guess what! We get them all the time. People are embarrassed.'

'He shouted and slammed the phone down on Mrs Murdoch when she asked when he was going to visit after the funeral." That's what happened to Pippa. She phoned to ask when next month's rotas would be ready, and he shouted at her.'

Chris outlined the options. There was a capability procedure if it was health-related, or mediation, or consultancy from the diocese. Both of them knew, however, that the problem was really disciplinary.

'I work in the NHS,' said Linda. 'If someone behaved like that at work something would be done about it. They'd be suspended. There'd be an investigation, and if they were drunk, they'd be given their cards.'

Serious Professional Misconduct, then. The Clergy Discipline Measure was the only option.

In any other job this kind of behaviour would indeed be a disciplinary matter. Chris would support Linda in putting together the statements, and it would all go to the bishop.

Chris downloaded the CDM forms and got Linda to provide a list of people who might be willing to make a statement. When it came to it, most of them were afraid of Jason's temper, and wouldn't put anything in writing. In the end four people made statements about services where Jason had smelt of drink in church, made lewd comments, shouted at people, or threatened them. Mrs Murdoch added hers, and the complaint was prepared to go in Linda's name.

The rules said that there were now 28 days during which the bishop would take advice from his senior legal officer as to whether the complaint was serious, and the complainant had a right to make it.

Four weeks to the day after submitting her complaint, Linda wondered what the post would bring. Perhaps the forms had taken a couple of days in the post on their way to the bishop.

A week later. Still nothing.

Three weeks.

Four weeks and Linda felt she must chase it somehow, and phoned Archdeacon Chris.

'Really?' he said. 'Leave it with me and I'll try and chase things up.'

The next month, a letter arrived from the Palace. The bishop explained that the complaint standing in her name would go in. There was now a set period of time in which he could investigate and see if the matter could be dealt with by him in his diocese.

A few weeks later, Jason met the bishop.

'Don't believe a word of it, Bishop,' he said. 'This is a spiritual warfare issue. Can't you see? There's a battle going on here. There's a clique – the three witches I call them – who are out to get me by fair means or foul. Linda's one of them. They spread all kinds of lies about me. The Bible says if they've got a complaint about me they should come and discuss it with me first. It's the Christian way. These bitches go behind my back to you. This is spiritual warfare. I'm not going to let the Devil get away with it.'

'Thank you, Jason,' said the bishop. 'Your evidence is rather different from theirs. I take it you won't be willing to accept a penalty from me? But you do understand this means the complaint may have to go to a tribunal?'

'Bring it on!' said Jason. 'You and I both know we're going to get persecution when we preach the gospel!'

The bishop understood what he was saying, but a disturbing smell came off Jason's clothing. One of those new trendy aftershaves - or drink? He feared he knew the answer.

Next St Barnabas PCC meeting was memorable. Not a word was said about any complaint, but Jason chose as his devotional text St Matthew 12:30-31:

> Whoever is not with me is against me, and whoever does not gather with me scatters. Therefore, I tell you, every sin and blasphemy will be forgiven people, but the blasphemy against the Spirit will not be forgiven.

'That's what's going on here!' said Jason. 'There are some spiteful gossiping bitches in this place. They know who they are. Soon I will, too. I'm on the job. I'll go and sort them out. So I'm telling you, as God is my witness, I'm going to close down all their nonsense. Those bitches can go to the bishop and try and get me sacked all they like. I'm God's man. They won't get away with it. If they don't like it, they know what they can do.'

Linda felt sick. Still, she told herself, the bishop knows the real story. If anyone can sort this mess out, he can.

Six months later, the investigating officer had been and gone.

As far as the complaint went, a very few people knew, but most didn't. Jason said nothing directly but had a way of looking down from the pulpit at the women he thought had complained. Jason had his supporters as well, of course. They said nothing because the fact there was a complaint going on was a secret, and if it got out others might join in. The investigating officer told Linda her complaint was being assessed by a retired high court judge.

Linda still believed the bishop. Surely a formal tribunal would sort things out. She was disturbed, though, when someone buttonholed her after church and said 'I wouldn't hold your breath. That bishop has just given Jason £2000 of clergy charity money "at this trying time".'

Six weeks later, former Lord Justice Peverell delivered his decision. There would be no tribunal. There was no appeal against the decision.

For a start, said the judgment, some of the statements related to behaviour alleged to have happened more than a year before the complaint had gone in. These could not be taken into consideration, as no application had been made to hear matters that were out of time. Many witnesses spoke of drunkenness, but some disputed this evidence. Therefore, no tribunal could decide the truth of the matter. Anyway, said the Judge, drunkenness and lewd language are upsetting, of course, but not serious enough to warrant action in and of themselves. There was obviously a serious pastoral breakdown at St Barnabas. Disciplinary action would be impractical and uneconomic. The solution would be pastoral not legal.

Linda showed the letter to her husband Colin. He was furious.

'So he gets away with it!' said Colin. 'Six of one and half a dozen of the other? He doesn't agree he should be punished, so let's not bother! A pastoral solution? What would that be? At long last His Lordship rules – Boys will be boys. It's disgusting!'

9. Muriel

Jonty loved growing up in Africa – Botswana to be precise. His mum was a doctor and dad was a Missionary with the African Overseas Missionary Society.

One Thursday his parents called him in.

'Jonty, we need to explain something to you. You remember last time we went home to England and stayed with Gramps? Well now Gramps says he will pay for you to go to a wonderful school there. It's got loads of great things to do, and you're bound to make really good new friends. People who go to Staplehurst count for something in life. You'll love it!'

Jonty wasn't so sure. He had all the friends he wanted already. He played every day with the other boys on the compound. He felt proud that his dad was the Minister in the big house.

He had a lovely long summer enjoying beautiful sunny days, and the freedom, and the wildlife, and fun with his African friends.

He didn't know how to talk about his growing apprehension. Mummy was always busy with her sick people, and Daddy had a traffic light system on his study door. Nobody was to enter except when the lights were green. He'd heard even Mummy being told off for that, so he knew better than to try.

The week before leaving for England, Mummy was reading him his story with prayers at bedtime. 'Mummy,

I love it here. Why do I have to go away? Don't you want me to stay with you?'

'Of course we do, darling. We'd love to keep you. But do you remember how God had a special plan for Joshua when he was nervous just like you. God said, "be strong and very courageous". And I know you can do that for us, and for God.'

'How do you mean, mummy?'

'Well, darling, the Lord has specially called Daddy to bring the good news of Jesus to people in Africa. If they don't hear all about Jesus how are they ever going to get to heaven? And if we had to come home for you to go to school, think of the sick people in my clinic. I wouldn't be able to help them any more.'

Jonty wasn't quite sure, but he knew God would look after him, and after all he was going back to England, and Daddy promised him 'We're closer to you than you think even when you're in England. Every time you pray, we'll pray and then we're all close to Jesus, and each other, in our hearts. The Lord never calls us to do anything special without giving us the strength to do it. It'll be the making of you, like it was for Gramps ....'

Walking across the field on his second day at Staplehurst, a voice bellowed out behind him 'Oy! Titch! Yes, you! New bugs don't walk across the Meadow. It's for Prefects!'

'I'm sorry,' said Jonty. 'I didn't know. I won't do it again!'

'Damn right you won't. Six rashers for you. Report to my study tomorrow at 8.'

Only Masters at Staplehurst could use the cane. Prefects gave what the boys called 'rashers' with gym shoes. Jonty felt utterly humiliated. He tried not to cry. He swore if he ever became a prefect he'd never pick on new bugs or give out rashers.

It never got any better. Jonty couldn't tell his mum how awful it was. Almost all the other boys had posh homes in England, and dads who drove smart cars. Their mums sent treats for their tuck boxes, and their daddies were rich people with big houses and important jobs.

They called Jonty 'Titch' for the next seven years. He hated it. He wasn't big enough to excel at games, but he learnt to survive, partly by making a joke of things. He learnt to pretend not to feel the hurt and humiliation. In the end he really couldn't feel anything any more. When he became a prefect, of course, he gave out rashers, just like all the others.

Food was rubbish at Theological College. Jonty joked that after 5 years at Staplehurst and then public school, it was a doddle.

Jonty's curacy went well, on the whole. His next job was a small suburban church, but then he landed the post of vicar of St Sam's, a city centre church in a university town with a thriving student ministry. He loved the pace of life there, and the way people responded to his teaching. Things grew, with a big building project, and before too long, there were ten staff. He saw himself as a strong leader. He didn't notice when some of the staff made a point of never being alone with him.

Jonty was mortified, then furious, when one morning an official complaint came through the door from the archdeacon. Apparently, he had been very rude to a woman called Muriel Oldbrook. He even had to think twice about who she was – some old trout from the 8.00 Prayer Book lot. It was like being back on the meadow at Staplehurst.

She had come in to help with midweek coffee when someone was on holiday and couldn't find the right supplies. She'd gone round to Sainsbury's in a tizz and bought instant coffee and teabags. Then she filled in an expenses claim from the office without anyone authorising it first.

When he found out, Jonty told her firmly that all church expenses had to be authorised properly in advance.

'How was I supposed to know that?' she said.

'Any fool would know that!' Jonty snapped.

'You can't speak to me like that, Vicar!'

'You don't seem to understand, we can't let just anyone order church supplies.'

'I don't like the way you're speaking to me, Vicar. I'm going to tell the churchwardens you shouted at me.'

'You do that, then!' shouted Jonty. 'But you stay away from communion until we've sorted you out.'

10. Ryan and Bethany

Ryan and Bethany met at MPower, the church youth group at St Joe's. They were only 16 and nobody particularly thought it would last, but incredibly it did, even after Ryan went to Cardiff and Bethany to Manchester.

'You've really got to work at a long-distance relationship,' said Bethany's mum. 'Dad and I had 6 months apart and we only just made it.'

'I know, Mum' said Bethany. 'But we've prayed about it and we've promised to make sure we see each other every month. We're expecting it to be tough, but if it's God's plan for us, it'll work out okay.'

Both got good degrees. Ryan got a 2:1, and Bethany a first. Speakers at both their graduations talked about their great achievements. But an even greater achievement, they felt, was managing to stay together all the way through uni.

Like many students both came back after graduation to the hotel of mum and dad. Bethany's parents actually had a granny flat that nobody used any more, so that was perfect. They were still together, and they threw themselves back into life at St Joe's. They even began to help out with a bit of Leadership at MPower.

Soon after there was an interregnum, during which,

like many St Joe's people, Ryan stepped up to the plate. He joined the PCC and took on extra leadership at MPower.

The new man, Jonathan, explained to the congregation early on that everybody actually called him Rufus. 'It all goes back to School. I did archery when I had an eyepatch from a rugger injury one term. The others called me Rufus and it kind of stuck!'

A few months later Rufus came back from his annual Leadership conference even more fired up than usual.

'We need to be a church that grows leaders,' he told the PCC. 'God's given me a Numbers 11 Vision!'

'What's one of those?' asked Ivy the verger.

'It's Numbers 11:29 of course,' said Rufus. 'Moses said, I wish that all the LORD's people were prophets and that the LORD would put his Spirit on them!' And the Lord said to me, "This is what I want for St Joe's, Rufus, and I know that's your passion too!" What I mean is, more than anything else, God wants to raise up new young leaders here for this generation.'

Ryan was really excited, and so was Bethany when he told her that evening. Next day he went to see Rufus to find out how he could be part of God's new vision for St Joe's.

'Well,' said the vicar, 'I wondered when you'd come and ask. God always has bigger plans for our lives than we do. It all comes down to discipleship – doing what he wants not what you want any more. I'm going to pray about this, but if you're up for the commitment, I could mentor you for a bit. Let's be open to the Spirit on this one ....'

Ryan loved being mentored every week by Rufus. He felt special and was learning awesome new things about God. After a couple of months Rufus phoned one day. 'It's terrific what God's doing here. I'm really thrilled for you, fella. I think the Lord may be opening some fantastic doors in your life. I was praying, and he said to me he wants you for the A-Team. Go away and please just pray about it?'

Ryan had only heard rumours about the A-Team. Someone called it Rufus's kitchen cabinet. Sure the church had a PCC and churchwardens and all that stuff, but the real spiritual work went on in the A-Team. Ryan was secretly flattered to be invited.

Bethany told Ryan how proud she was of him, but secretly she was sorry if this was going to mean less time for each other. A-Team Training happened on Saturday mornings. She and Ryan had busy lives and their park run was their catch-up time.

Things came to a bit of a head when Bethany's sister got married on the same weekend as the A-Team was running the MPower house party. She felt really let down when Ryan didn't even try to get out of it.

A few weeks later, Rufus was preaching on David. The text was 2 Samuel 6. 'David danced before the ark with all his might as it was being brought to Jerusalem,' said Rufus. 'Good news means joy, of course. That's what we aim for here. But there's bad news too. In verse 6 this man called Uzzah dared to touch the ark. He was only trying to steady it, but look, it says "God's anger was kindled against him and the Lord struck him down dead". That will sound harsh to secular people. Even I find it bit shocking. But it's a warning. Secular logic isn't enough. If we really mean business with God, we have to take Scripture seriously.

'It's a sad fact, but even in a church like St Joe's there are people who are just not fully committed. They love what we do here, but they're not prepared to pay the price. They seem to think just because people enjoy themselves here it's basically a social club. God says that's just not good enough. Only a few weeks ago, we took some of our key young people away to firm up things with the Lord. Ryan and the A-Team did a brilliant job in spite of the fact that someone thought he should have gone to a family social event instead. Jesus says anyone who loves the family more than him isn't fit for the kingdom ....'

Later that day, Bethany cornered Ryan. 'We've got to talk, babe.'

'Really? What about?'

'I was gutted this morning in church. What Rufus said about me and Laura's wedding was way out of order – and in the sermon. Everybody knows he was talking about me. What else do you tell him? Do you talk about our sex life?'

'You don't understand. We have to be fully discipled for A-Team Training. We share everything. So yes, of course he knew, but I didn't think he'd put it in the sermon.'

'You seem to spend all your time with Rufus. Why don't you move in with him – just the two of you? Then you could tell him everything.'

'So now we get the truth, Bethany. You really are one of those people who just string along for the show. I've always stood up for you. Rufus thinks we're unequally yoked. You know. What Paul said about not marrying unbelievers. Seems he's got a point ....'

11. Jane

Ministry Development Review time was coming round again. Helen loved being a bishop's reviewer. It meant meeting three members of the clergy a year and helping them reflect on their work. She was really impressed by the commitment and sincerity of her reviewees – none of them saints, perhaps, but all good and decent people trying their best to follow a difficult calling and keep the plates spinning.

Jane was the last of this year's crop.

Helen liked Jane. It very hard not to like her, with her funny sweaters with sheep on, green highlights and her labradoodle called Chocolate. Reading her preparation form, Helen felt this had been as good a year as any.

There were still tensions among Jane's six parishes, of

course, and one or two difficult characters about, but Jane's confidence seemed to be growing. Outside the world of work, she had the dog, her pilates, holidays with friends in north Wales, and an annual retreat. She got on with her spiritual director, and had attended an interesting workshop on the Enneagram, a tool for spiritual and personal discernment. School assemblies were often the highlight of her week, and there had been a couple of major flower festivals, along with an appearance on local radio. Jane felt she could do with a sabbatical, but couldn't see how to make it happen and was worried about the dog and the extra work she'd have to do arranging it and getting it past the sabbaticals committee. Numbers were slightly down, but weren't they everywhere?

For their first half hour together, all went much as expected. The person in front of Helen matched up well with the person on the form. With things well warmed up, Helen thought the time might have come for some gentle challenge.

'How are you doing with Thy Will be Done?' she asked.

'Bit of a curate's egg,' said Jane. I like the focus on prayer. I really do, but I can't get away from the feeling that the whole course is really all about numbers. The archbishop put that thing around last year saying poor numbers are down to poor leadership. I think he probably meant me, not him.'

'How do you mean?' asked Helen.

'Well I try and try, but nothing I do seems to be enough. Old people die and move away. I'm not killing them, honestly! But the numbers are down, and I can't think what to do about it. If I try new things the old guard kick up. If I don't, new people say it's too boring for them. We get children at school services, but if I try anything like that on a Sunday morning the parents aren't too keen and, worse still, the old guard moan about the noise in church. I just can't win!'

'What support have you got?' asked Helen.

'Support? You must be joking! The diocese talks the talk about support, but all I get from them are complaints about the quota and faculty forms. The last straw came through the letterbox yesterday. Please don't tell anyone, but the archdeacon has taken out a CDM against me. I didn't sleep a wink last night, worrying about it.'

'What exactly is a CDM?' asked Helen

'It's a formal complaint.'

'Whatever are you supposed to have done?'

'Nothing!' said Jane. 'I don't think I've done anything wrong. I've always given everything in ministry. Now that doesn't seem to be enough any more ....' Her voice trailed away into sobs.

Helen wasn't sure whether she should open up what was obviously a major can of worms. But she didn't see how she could avoid it now. She offered Jane a tissue.

'All I did was try to help!' said Jane between tears. 'Jesus wouldn't have turned Amina away, so I didn't'

'And?' said Helen

'Well they're saying I didn't conduct a proper risk assessment when I invited her and her kids to stay while they looked for somewhere. I didn't check her immigration status like I should have. It was only going to be a day or so. It's not my fault. I went to the archdeacon for help, and look what I got – a CDM!'

'But surely you were only trying to be Christian,' suggested Helen.

'Of course!' said Jane. 'How was I to know Amina was illegal? I'm not a copper. I'm not an immigration officer. I'm a vicar. I didn't know what to do when the police turned up on my doorstep. That's why I phoned the archdeacon. I only wanted some advice. All the diocese seemed to care about was keeping it all out of the papers. And now they're saying I was unprofessional. I feel they've marked my cards ever since I did the service for Tony and Dave last year.'

'Tony and Dave?'

'They look after the churchyard at St Agnes. They got married in Barbados and wanted something in church afterwards. I didn't know what to do, so I phoned the archdeacon. He said it was my job to do something appropriate and pastoral, but he wasn't allowed to tell me what that might be. I did my best. Dave and Tony were fine about it. I thought the congregation would kick up, but they didn't. Gladys actually pulled me aside and thanked me. She said her grandson Grant was gay and she was right behind him and Jesus wouldn't mind gay people.'

'And?'

'And the vicar next door complained that I was blessing gay marriages, and ever since I feel they see me differently in the diocese. So now this feels like their way of getting back at me, and I can't bear it! To be honest, I don't know whether I want to work for people like that much longer. If I didn't have Chocolate I sometimes don't think I could carry on, I really don't ....'

After Helen had helped Jane get herself back together again with tea and chocolate digestives, she saw her reviewee on her way. She felt completely helpless. She just didn't know what to do, and the neat little feedback form about training and development wasn't helping. Obviously, Jane was a conscientious minister trying her best to do an impossible job. She couldn't help thinking in some ways she was her own worst enemy – could you be too good a priest?

12. Jennifer

Doctors say many patients only disclose the big issue as they're leaving the surgery. Martin was nearing the end of his shift on the Samaritans switchboard. He felt he'd been able to help Jennifer achieve a bit more perspective about her marriage breakup. She'd talked of suicide. She said one day soon she'd jump from the church tower. Then she brought up the thought again, almost in passing.

'One Sunday morning, I'll go there when they're all getting ready to pray. That's when I'll do it. That's when they'll begin to understand what they did to me.'

'Do you want to talk about it?' asked Martin

Years ago, Jennifer had been a teenager in the choir. All the girls talked about Mr Granger the organist. 'You don't want organ lessons from him,' they said. 'You'll get more than you bargained for.'

One choir trip, Granger made his move. She felt dirty, and guilty, especially when her Auntie Noreen said, 'Men are like that. You must have led him on.' She'd gone to see Tony, the vicar. She liked him and trusted him. He was a vicar after all. His kind of help was worse than Mr Granger's. Tony counselled her at the vicarage every few weeks, but it wasn't long before their meetings turned into more than that.

'Let's make this our special secret,' he said.

'I'll tell my mum on you!' she said, in a way Tony thought was playful. 'Please do,' said Tony. 'Nobody's going to believe you anyway....'

So she never did. What had happened in church remained in church for twenty-five years. It was only when her marriage to Craig began to break up, everything resurfaced. She couldn't bring herself to tell the couples counsellor, but she did talk to Hayley, her friend at work.

'You've got to tell someone about it now,' Hayley said. You'll never get any rest till you do.'

'Yes, but who?'

'I'd go to the top. Phone the bishop. He's supposed to be in charge.' Jennifer got the number off the diocesan website. She didn't get to speak to the bishop himself, but spoke to Claire, his chaplain. 'That's awful!' said Claire, and they were on the phone for over an hour. Claire seemed to care and to understand. When she put the phone down, Jennifer was sure something would happen. She just had to put the whole thing in writing, and it would be dealt with.

It wasn't an easy letter to write, and it took weeks. Jennifer didn't know how much or how little to say. In the end she tried to get it all down on paper, everything. Writing it down brought it all back. It wasn't the sort of thing she could discuss with the children and Craig was gone. In the end she managed. She popped her letter in the box with considerable relief.

For the next few weeks, she checked the post immediately when she came in from work, but there was nothing. After six weeks she knew she had to phone Claire again.

'I'm sorry to say Tony died three years ago,' said Claire. 'I shouldn't really be telling you, but we're going to check our files here for all past cases. It's being done by a very senior social worker and if we find anything, we'll tell you. In the meantime, I'm sure your local church will support you.'

Jennifer felt more and more desperate as time passed by. Nothing seemed to be happening. She was losing sleep at nights. What she'd written in her letter went round and round in her head until it became so vivid it could have happened yesterday.

Before long she was called in by her supervisor, to say her job was now on the line. Lateness, lack of concentration and sloppy mistakes were unacceptable. If she wanted counselling, her supervisor hoped the doctor could help, but things couldn't go on like this.

'You've got to do something,' said Hayley. 'Sue them or something. Someone's got to be responsible for what they did to you. Even if he's dead, it happened in church and they've done nothing to help you.'

Now Jennifer began to notice adverts on the radio for lawyers who dealt with personal injury claims.

'Have you had an accident at work that wasn't your fault? We can help. No win, no fee.'

After a few days dithering, Jennifer phoned the 0800 number.

'I've tried to do it their way. Now I need your help!' she told the lawyer.

'We'll write to the bishop,' he said. 'We'll state your claim and ask them what they intend to do about it. If the answer's nothing, we may have to go to court. But don't worry. I'm sure they're insured, and their company will have to pay up.'

'It's not really about the money,' said Jennifer. 'Someone should take responsibility, that's all. I want a real apology, and a counsellor who can help me where it's messing up my mind.'

Three weeks later Jennifer found herself back in the solicitor's office. 'It's good news, kind of,' he told her. 'We can't bring a case because the vicar's dead. There is a legal principle called "vicarious liability" but it's being argued in the courts and, quite honestly, I'm not sure it will help you. I have heard from their solicitor, though, and he says they're willing to write a letter of apology and pay for your counselling. They can also make what's called an *ex gratia* payment for your distress. They've offered £10,000. You'll get £7,500 of that. Quite honestly it's probably the best we can do for you.'

The letter from the bishop seemed genuine and kind. He was appalled by what had happened and wanted to say on behalf of the Church how ashamed he felt. Of course this wasn't about money, but he hoped the coming payment would help her. He assured her that standards were much higher nowadays. All dioceses employed safeguarding advisers, and every member of the clergy had training. He would do everything in his power to ensure that no other teenager would suffer in future as she had. He sent every good wish and blessing.

Jennifer was glad to receive some money. She had lost her job and needed every penny for herself and the children. Living on benefits was no breeze. The whole system was degrading, and she hoped she would have a job by the time her money ran out. As she wrote applications, she began to realise her confidence was almost destroyed. She still felt slimed and dirty.

Maybe counselling would help. The surgery knew a good psychotherapist who worked with survivors of abuse. There would be six assessment meetings, then probably one a month for up to two years. The cost would be £110 an hour – £660 for the assessment, then up to £2400. Thank goodness, the Church was going to pay.

Jennifer was more optimistic than she'd been for a long time after her first assessment meeting. It wouldn't be easy, but Moira the counsellor seemed to know what she was doing. Five meetings later she felt very positive. It wasn't magic, but seeing Moira had made her realise how much she had to talk through. She was beginning to believe in herself again.

After a few sessions Moira tactfully said, 'I'll send the bill to the Church, shall I?'

A month later, Jennifer received a phone call from her counsellor. 'I'm really sorry, but there's something outstanding on your account. The Church has paid £500 and said that's their upper limit. We'll need to find someone else to pay. I wonder whether the surgery can help?'

They couldn't. Jennifer phoned Claire to plead with her. 'Look, Moira is actually making a difference. I'm getting my confidence back. You can't just leave me high and dry.'

'I'll have a word with the diocesan secretary,' said Claire.

Next day Claire phoned back. It was a difficult conversation. 'I've asked but I'm afraid there's really no wriggle room. The diocese has a £500 limit for counselling, even for clergy.' She could not bring herself to quote all he had said – 'That mad woman? It's £500. She'll just have to accept that's the way we do it.'

'So where does that leave me?' Jenifer asked Martin at the Samaritans. 'I've lost everything. I've got no job, and it looks as though I may lose my flat. The money they gave me is running out and the only person who's really helped me is Moira. Now I'm losing her too. What have I got to live for?'

13. Dan and Yvette

It shook the whole church community at St Anselm's when baby Connor died – it was a 'cot death', so sudden.

Dan and Yvette had had three cycles of IVF, and everyone was thrilled for them when Connor arrived. They made a huge fuss of him in church, with his cheeky smile and shock of golden hair.

It was a very difficult funeral, taking place only weeks after his christening. Alison the vicar spent a lot of time with the family preparing for the ordeal.

There was something especially tragic about Dan walking up the aisle, carrying the little white box. Yvette, fighting back tears, tenderly placed a single white rose on the coffin before it was finally lowered into the ground.

A fortnight later Alison called round to see how they were coping. Everyone had been marvellous, but it still seemed unreal. The funeral director had been asking them about the memorial. It would be a few weeks yet before the grave settled.

Days later, Alison, Dan and Yvette met in church and went out together to the 'Babies Row' in the churchyard – a line of tiny graves along the path, many bearing sad little mementos, teddy bears, footballs and solar powered nightlights. Some of the stones had touching inscriptions. Dan and Yvette wanted to keep it simple, though. One stood out for them – simply the baby's name, and the words 'Forever in our hearts. Safe with Jesus'.

'That's exactly what we want for Connor,' said Yvette. 'And gold letters, please – his golden hair is what everyone remembers about him.'

There was paperwork, but the funeral directors prepared everything. There was a small drawing, the inscription with gold lettering, the dimensions and specifications.

'What does it mean when it says 'Semi-polished?' Yvette asked Alison.

'Well, it's a bit silly really,' said the vicar, 'but there's a church official called the Chancellor. She has the last word about gravestones – it's a bit like planning permission – and she won't allow polished stone. But if the Stonemasons call it 'semi-polished' that seems to do the trick.'

Alison signed off on the stone. It would be ready in six weeks, so then they could have a few prayers for Connor round the grave.

Next week Alison took her curate to the Diocesan Offices for a training day about funerals. They brought Connor's funeral as a case study, and everybody found it helpful to think through how they could handle such a tragic pastoral situation.

In the afternoon, Howard, the bright young assistant registrar, came to do an hour on the new churchyard regulations.

'It's amazing what people think goes on graves!' he said. 'They'd be sticking garden gnomes on them if we let them. Now there aren't many changes, but please bear in mind Veronica's tightening things up a bit.'

'What about semi-polished stone?' asked Alison.

'Well, it's a grey area but I don't see how you can stop that,' said Howard.

'Oh no!' said John, Alison's curate. 'Page 5 says, "Lettering may be uncoloured, grey or black only". What's that about?'

'Oh, that one!' said Howard. People want all kinds of tacky colours, red, blue, even gold. Veronica thinks it's vulgar. So she's written it into the new regulations – black only.'

'That's me done for, then,' said Alison. 'I've just signed off a baby's grave with gold lettering. It's what they really wanted. What can I do?'

'In theory,' said Howard, 'you could kick it upstairs. A Consistory Court could allow it. It would cost a few bob, and, quite honestly it would be a waste of the parents' time and money. It's very much a red line for Veronica. She's been trying to stamp it out for years. There's no way she'll roll over on this one.'

'Sod that!' said Alison to John in the car going home. 'I can't go back to them and say that ....'

14. Norman

When Daniel died, Norman was devastated. They'd been together for more than thirty years. The funeral director asked Norman whether he wanted a minister.

What a question!

Norman was brought up as a strong Christian in his local church but in his teenage years he realised he was gay. The matter was studiously cloaked in silence at St Peter's until, in his twenties, he moved in with Daniel.

Soon afterwards, Derek the vicar came round.

'Of course everyone is welcome at St Peter's, but God's word is unambiguous about homosexuality. I can't go on giving someone like you communion as long as you are openly living together as a couple. God is a holy God. We all know what he thinks of this sort of thing. We are called to love the sinner, but hate the sin. It's the only way to give homosexuals any hope. If we decide to live God's way, he gives us the power to be the people he wants us to be.'

Norman froze. He was being thrown out of his church, in his own front room, with Daniel coming home any minute. He was angry and humiliated all at once. He knew he would never darken church doors again, least of all St Peter's.

But now Daniel was dead, and Norman wanted to do the right thing. As long as the minister wasn't Derek. 'It won't be,' said the Funeral Director. 'He was four vicars ago!' Having a real minister really did seem like the right thing to do.

The funeral went well in the circumstances. When Brian the vicar came round to visit a week later Norman was pleasantly surprised. It was helpful to have a friendly listening ear, and at the funeral Brian had spoken kindly, even movingly, of their relationship, and the love they had shared for thirty years.

Towards the end of the visit, Norman began to warm towards Brian and even began to think of him as a friend.

'I can see St Peter's was a very important part of your life,' said Brian. 'We'd love to see you back again any time you could manage. I bet that there'll still be people who remember you.'

'I vowed I'd never go to your church ever again after what Derek did to us,' said Norman. 'He made it sound as though we were sinful and dirty. We knew our love was the best thing that ever happened to either of us. Whatever that bloody man said about us, he had no right to load us with shame and guilt. We knew what we had together was beautiful.'

'I understand,' said Brian. 'I'm so sorry about what happened to you. Some St Peter's folk take a traditional view of human sexuality, of course. That's their right, but we've come a long way since then in the Church. I've been on a journey myself. I don't tell people because that would be divisive. The Church really does recognise gay people's relationships now. Of course they can be fabulous, like you and Daniel. The archbishop said exactly that the other day. He knows great gay couples. I'm sure we'd all love to see you again anytime.'

A year later, Norman felt he was actually getting his faith and his church back. He was going most weeks. He was making new friends. Life still felt empty without Daniel but having a home group with whom he could pray and talk things over helped. It felt very healing when he was elected as a sidesman at the annual meeting. It seemed Brian was right. The Church really had changed.

Prayer ministry was offered after every service at St Peter's. One icy winter he slipped on a path and almost broke his wrist. It was still sore, and he thought he'd go up and be prayed for.

'We'd love to pray for you, Norman!' said Phil, the prayer minister. 'Actually, I've been wondering when you'd come up for prayer. It's wonderful what God can do for same-sex attracted people. They often think it's hopeless, But God knows best!' Norman didn't like the sound of this. He liked it even less when the whole healing prayer group gathered round him and began to stretch out their hands.

'Now, Norman,' said Phil, 'we just want to pray for you for healing. God is a God of new beginnings, and we're all sinners. May we do that now?'

'No, Phil,' said Norman firmly. 'I don't want you to pray for me. Not like that. Being me isn't a disease. I'm not sick. I don't need your kind of healing.'

'Okay, Norman. Of course it's very hard for you. Same-sex attraction isn't easy. Don't worry. We'll be praying for you anyway, and when you're ready ....'

Norman didn't feel like going to church the next week,

but he was on the rota. The preacher was the church's Link Missionary.

'We know how tough your spiritual battle has become in England,' he said. 'There are so many people who want to normalise homosexual lifestyles. Same-sex-attracted males will tell you they can't help it, just like drunkards and thieves, even paedophiles. They know the things they do are sinful. What do we do? We pray for sinners, but if we really love them, we owe it to them and the Lord to tell it straight. Orthodox Christians are under attack from the homosexualist lobby. Our church says "Enough!" Thank you for standing alongside us.'

Norman felt sick. He walked sadly out of church, knowing he'd never be back.

15. Lucy

Lucy was surprised when Roy, her Diocesan Director of Ordinands, suggested she go and visit St Vincent's as a possibility for her training. It did not particularly affirm women priests but, Roy said, 'It's important to explore all your options. They say they're keen to have more women. You just never know.'

'How many female students do you actually have?' she asked the Senior Tutor.

'Well, just one at the moment,' he said. 'But we do feel we rather miss out. We could do with a woman's touch around here.'

That evening after chapel, Lucy wandered down for a drink.

Alistair stood out from the other students in the bar. He was taller and stockier, and seemed less introverted than the others. Ten years ago he had played in the GB Under-23 hockey squad he told her.

'What a coincidence,' said Lucy. 'So did my brother Hugh. Last year. You won't know him, of course ....'

Much to her surprise Lucy found she was rather enjoying herself, but it had been a long day, and it was time to turn in. Alistair offered to help with her bags and show her the way to her guest room. It was on the third floor.

'Thanks, Alistair. See you at breakfast!' she said.

'Don't I get a goodnight kiss?' he said.

Alistair wouldn't take no for an answer. After twenty minutes of drunken groping, somehow, she got him out of the room. She was shaking as she locked the door.

Next morning she was still shaking. After morning chapel she went to the principal to report what had happened.

'I'm so very sorry to hear this. I think he's let himself down very badly. This isn't the sort of thing we expect from a Vincentian. What would you like us to do?'

'Police?' she said. 'Or is there some university thing you're meant to do?'

'Leave it with us. We take this sort of thing very seriously, I can assure you. We'll deal with him. I should let your diocese know, and your DDO will look after you pastorally.'

Lucy's meeting with Roy was an ordeal, but he was kind and listened well.

'I nearly went to the police,' she said. 'But the principal assured me it would be dealt with properly. That means privately, doesn't it? I really don't want this to get around.'

'Of course not!' said Roy. 'I quite understand. Leave it with me.'

It was Lucy's third year of ordination training at St Gabriel's. She had enjoyed training, on the whole. She rarely thought about what had happened with Alistair. The third years were devising a liturgy for survivors of Church abuse. Another student, Bob, was the team leader on the project.

'Let's get a few of us together,' he said. 'Lucy, you'll

want to join us. You've got a thing or two to say about this, I'm sure.'

'What do you mean?' she asked.

'Well the Alistair thing at St Vincent's of course. They sent him down, didn't they?'

'What!' said Lucy. 'How did you know about that! It's personal! Roy promised me!'

'I'm so sorry, Lucy!' said Bob. 'Gill told me. I thought everyone knew!'

Lucy was furious when she phoned Roy next day.

'I trusted you!' she shouted. 'You said a note would go on my file and everything would be dealt with confidentially. Now it looks as though everyone knows. What you've done to me feels almost as bad as Alistair.'

'I'm sorry, Lucy,' said Roy. 'Various people needed to know at the time, of course. We looked into what happened very carefully. We dealt with it. I hardly think you're being fair when you compare me with Alistair. What he did was deeply, deeply wrong. But if I may say so, we are dealing with a few problems we wouldn't have if ordinands' dress standards were higher. If I were you, I'd tone it down a bit in future ....'

2
Why Pass By?

These miniatures make very uncomfortable reading because of the deep pain and suffering they reflect, sometimes experienced over many years. The severe pain of the original abuse has often been compounded by the Church's response or lack of it. It seems cruel and heartless behaviour from a community that claims to be good news, based on Jesus' great command

> to love the Lord your God with all your heart and with all your soul and with all your mind and with all your strength, and love your neighbour as yourself. (Luke 10:27)

This foundational command is the litmus test of authentic faith. Our neighbours who are survivors do not experience being loved. They experience, each in a particular way, something that leaves them outside that circle of love which Jesus says is all-embracing.

It can be tempting to consider this command of Jesus as a touchy-feely dynamic of our faith, not exactly optional, but less central than the hard-core stuff of doctrine and order. Nothing could be further from the truth. Failing to live by this command undermines anything else we might attempt to do. It throws into question the truth of the whole enterprise. If faith becomes less than Jesus' radical, transformative, all-inclusive love, all that remains is white noise in a hollow echo chamber. St Paul recognises this in 1 Corinthians 13:1:

> If I speak in the tongues of human beings and of angels but

do not have love, I have become a sounding bronze or a cymbal clashing.

This fundamental of love is what the Church is about, what the Church invites people to experience, what it proclaims as the way God heals and restores us. Because of this very high and wonderful ideal we are drawn to the Church, often as wounded people looking for exactly that unconditionality. We trust the people we encounter and have high expectations of love and acceptance.

It is obvious that no individual church or organisation can possibly live up to such an ideal. There will be those who come inside the tent for the very reason that a high level of trust allows them to abuse and violate others in the most horrific ways. The Church, above all institutions, is expected to understand the theological territory within which abuse happens. The recently exposed John Smyth (Iwerne Camps) abuse and Bishop Peter Ball's crimes had very particular theological micro-climates to normalise abnormal behaviour.

Theology can heal, but it can also hurt. Ioannis Athanasiou, Safeguarding Lead for the United Reformed Church points out:

> You cannot understand safeguarding if you take it out of its theological context.

One survivor of serious domestic abuse left the room after many hours of telling their story with the parting shot: 'It was the theology that did it you know.' Her abusive husband had used Scripture against her to underpin violent actions.

The primary focus of this book is the response of the Church once abuse has happened, but it does seem that some powerful theological stories and cultures normalise and even idealise the most extraordinary and abhorrent behaviour.

At one level the Church has worked hard to develop systems and processes to try to prevent recurrence. Every time a new story comes into the public domain a new tranche of process is devised so that the Church can legitimately say 'That was then – now we do things better'.

This sort of administrative response is the easy bit. It is only a small part, however, of a truly humane and Christian response to those who have been abused. People naturally expect professional guardians of the faith to be quick to draw alongside the wounded and do whatever it takes to help them heal and rebuild their lives. Despite best intentions all too often this does not happen. Those who speak loudest about the love of God often treat survivors as a threat to the institution. They will not spend money to put any meat on the dry bones of their apologies, nor spend time getting alongside them. Being in the same room as survivors at a General Synod fringe meeting in July 2018, far from evoking compassion in some of the bishops present, actually provoked anger.

This is not a call for perfection. We expect the Church to be imperfect. Jesus has extraordinary compassion for people who make a mess of things. Forgiveness and healing ooze out of his every pore. The only exception is his attitude to hypocrisy. He loudly condemned men (and of course it was men in those days) who claim to be speaking in the God's name, yet behave in ways that take life from people rather than giving it.

Hypocrisy has always been the Church's greatest vulnerability. It broke Jesus' heart and it made him angry. The story about the cleansing of the Temple (Matthew 21:12-17) isn't an anti-capitalist rant about trading activities on holy ground. The traders concerned may understandably have felt aggrieved about his anger. They were not running a secular gift shop, but resourcing the core requirements of the place. Yet he accused them of turning a house of prayer into a den of thieves. When what was preached fell out of sync with what was being done, it stirred his anger.

No wonder, then, that Jesus had a difficult relationship with religious professionals. He told parables that exposed them to ridicule and they spied on him to accumulate damning evidence. He refused to be taken in by their displays of piety:

> The scribes and the Pharisees sit on Moses' seat; therefore, do whatever they teach you and follow it; but do not do as they do, for they do not practise what they teach. (Matthew 23:2-3)

All four gospels describe high tension between Jesus and the scribes and Pharisees. The most pointed of his warnings about them are traditionally called the 'Woes of the Pharisees'. Jesus' language about them becomes intense and florid. His searing critique echoes throughout the gospels. It must have resonated powerfully for it to have been so well documented.

By no means were all scribes and Pharisees hypocrites. Nicodemus was a Pharisee and a member of the Sanhedrin. The three mentions we have in John's gospel speak of a man who was open minded, refusing to go along with the groupthink of his fellow leaders, visiting Jesus by night to hear for himself. Nicodemus the Pharisee also had a high ethic of justice, reminding his colleagues in John 7:50-51 that the law required a fair hearing before judging anyone. We know Nicodemus to have had a compassionate and generous heart, providing the necessary embalming spices and assisting in Jesus' burial. He seems to have been an honourable Pharisee.

Gamaliel, Paul's early instructor, could have been amongst those chief rulers mentioned in John 12:42 - 43 who secretly believed in Christ. He had a reputation for scholarship and the deepest integrity. He was also an advocate for women and non-Jews. In Acts 22:3 Paul referred to Gamaliel, to demonstrate the quality of his own early learning – 'I am a Jew ... brought up ... at the feet of Gamaliel'. He was held in such high regard that the Talmud records 'When Rabban Gamaliel the Elder died, regard for the Torah ceased, and purity and piety died.'

It is clear, then, that some scribes and Pharisees did not sacrifice their integrity for the sake of their religion, but Jesus encountered plenty who did and his words to them are tough. Reading them in the twenty-first century, it is sadly not that difficult to populate each woe with its modern equivalent. When we do, red warning lights come on.

> They tie up heavy burdens, hard to bear, and lay them on the shoulders of others; but they themselves are unwilling to lift a finger to move them.
>
> They do all their deeds to be seen by others; for they make their phylacteries broad and their fringes long.
>
> They love to have the place of honor at banquets and the best seats in the synagogues, and to be greeted with respect in the marketplaces, and to have people call them rabbi ...
>
> But woe to you, scribes and Pharisees, hypocrites! For you lock people out of the kingdom of heaven. For you do not go in yourselves, and when others are going in, you stop them. Woe to you, scribes and Pharisees, hypocrites! For you cross sea and land to make a single convert, and you make the new convert twice as much a child of hell as yourselves.
>
> Woe to you, blind guides, who say, 'Whoever swears by the sanctuary is bound by nothing, but whoever swears by the gold of the sanctuary is bound by the oath.' You blind fools! For which is greater, the gold or the sanctuary that has made the gold sacred? And you say, 'Whoever swears by the altar is bound by nothing, but whoever swears by the gift that is on the altar is bound by the oath.' How blind you

are! For which is greater, the gift or the altar that makes the gift sacred? So whoever swears by the altar, swears by it and by everything on it; and whoever swears by the sanctuary, swears by it and by the one who dwells in it; and whoever swears by heaven, swears by the throne of God and by the one who is seated upon it.

Woe to you, scribes and Pharisees, hypocrites! For you tithe mint, dill, and cummin, and have neglected the weightier matters of the law: justice and mercy and faith. It is these you ought to have practiced without neglecting the others. You blind guides! You strain out a gnat but swallow a camel!

Woe to you, scribes and Pharisees, hypocrites! For you clean the outside of the cup and of the plate, but inside they are full of greed and self-indulgence. You blind Pharisee! First clean the inside of the cup, so that the outside also may become clean.

Woe to you, scribes and Pharisees, hypocrites! For you are like whitewashed tombs, which on the outside look beautiful, but inside they are full of the bones of the dead and of all kinds of filth. So you also on the outside look righteous to others, but inside you are full of hypocrisy and lawlessness.

Woe to you, scribes and Pharisees, hypocrites! For you build the tombs of the prophets and decorate the graves of the righteous, and you say, 'If we had lived in the days of our ancestors, we would not have taken part with them in shedding the blood of the prophets.' Thus you testify against yourselves that you are descendants of those who murdered the prophets. Fill up, then, the measure of your ancestors.

You snakes, you brood of vipers! How can you escape being sentenced to hell? (Matthew 23: 4-8, 13-33)

This is a multi-layered text. Jesus puts the disconnect between what the scribes and Pharisees teach and the reality of their lives under very precise scrutiny. His analysis is devastating. Not only are they mere shells of the men of faith they purport to be, but they damage the lives of others by imposing rules and regulations that they themselves fail to observe. It's all there – abuse of power, lack of alignment, secrecy, hunger for status and wealth.

Matthew 23 and parallel texts (Luke 11:39-52 and Mark 7:1-23) are firstly of course about the flesh and blood scribes and Pharisees that Jesus saw day by day. They were plotting to murder him, motivated largely by the fact that he saw right through them and showed them up for what they were. They took offence because his loving, life-giving, inclusive message underlined how dark and lifeless they had become.

Jesus' words resonate as powerfully today as when they were first heard. One striking example of this resonance comes from Pope Francis, in his traditional Christmas greeting to the Curia in 2014:

> The Argentinian pontiff used a traditional Christmas greeting on Monday to the cardinals, bishops and priests who run the Holy See to portray a church hierarchy that had lost its humanity at times, a body consumed by narcissism and excessive activity, where men who are meant to serve God with optimism instead presented a hardened, sterile face to the world. (*Guardian*, 22 December 2014)

Reflecting, surely, the woes of the Pharisees, Pope Francis went on to list 15 'ailments of the Curia'. These ring horribly true of all religions that prioritise the flourishing of the institution over the flourishing of people. The Pope's words demonstrate that the abusive behaviours in our stories in the previous chapter, have deep roots in exactly this kind of inward looking, self-serving and hypocritical way of doing religion.

1. *Feeling immortal, immune or indispensable.* 'A Curia that doesn't criticise itself, that doesn't update itself, that doesn't seek to improve itself is a sick body.' In the first story about Mark (1), not only did his original abuser feel immune, but his feeling was proved right as others in the hierarchy acted in totally unaccountable ways. They were unable to imagine one of their own being culpable. They responded to his need with inaccuracies and boys' room backchat, and thus failed Mark over many decades.

2. *Working too hard.* 'Rest for those who have done their work is necessary, good and should be taken seriously.' The work ethic of many churches and priests is fertile ground for abuse. Training incumbents can be slave drivers for curates like Geoff (4). The conscientious vicar Jane (11) ends up in trouble for being too Christian in her response to a homeless person. All too often, the Church preaches grace but lives by works. The expectations of the leaders, the parish or indeed the person themselves can lead to a driven ministry that is deeply unhealthy.

3. *Becoming spiritually and mentally hardened.* 'It's dangerous to lose that human sensibility that lets you cry with those who are crying, and celebrate those who are joyful.' For Jennifer (12) to find healing she needed counselling. Her need calls for human generosity, but was met by a crushing and inhuman offer of a paltry £500. Dan and Yvette (13) also have needs arising from the death of their child that call for a gentle pastoral response not a cold administrative brick wall.

4. *Planning too much.* 'Preparing things well is necessary,

but don't fall into the temptation of trying to close or direct the freedom of the Holy Spirit, which is bigger and more generous than any human plan.' Geoff (7) was responsive to the Remembrance Day liturgy and handled it very well. Sally, his training incumbent, had lost the ability to see that, and crushed him with her criticism.

5. **Working without coordination, like an orchestra that produces noise.** *'When the foot tells the hand, "I don't need you" or the hand tells the head "I'm in charge".* So many people who feel re-abused by the Church's actions experience exactly this. Lucy (8) experiences her personal information being inappropriately shared despite assurances that it would be kept private. Norman (14) was told one thing by his vicar in private and was then humiliated from the pulpit by a guest speaker that the same vicar had invited.

6. **Having 'spiritual Alzheimer's'.** *'We see it in the people who have forgotten their encounter with the Lord ... in those who depend completely on their here and now, on their passions, whims and manias, in those who build walls around themselves and become enslaved to the idols that they have built with their own hands.'* Abusers in church show an uncanny ability to compartmentalise faith and action. The highest spirituality seemingly coexists quite happily with the lowest abuse. Mark's original abuser (1) does this, but it emerges that others in the hierarchy have grown into a version of their role which leaves them so detached from their original faith, as well as Mark's reality, that they are unable to do the right thing. Malcolm (6) is bullied by Barry, his church Treasurer. The way Barry uses power and control is far removed from

the Church's values, but can no longer be challenged because of the fear he generates in others.

7. *'Being rivals or boastful ... When one's appearance, the colour of one's vestments or honorific titles become the primary objective of life.'* Sadly Geoff's (7) story is classic. Training incumbents can experience their curates as a threat, leading them to abuse their power. There is an extra spiritual twist to this in traditions whose understanding of authority make Priests seem above criticism.

8. *Suffering from 'existential schizophrenia'. 'It's the sickness of those who live a double life, fruit of hypocrisy that is typical of mediocre and progressive spiritual emptiness that academic degrees cannot fill. It's a sickness that often affects those who, abandoning pastoral service, limit themselves to bureaucratic work, losing contact with reality and concrete people.'* In a very sad way Peter (12) has filled his life with a successful career as a barrister and when he has to face a spiritual choice and tell what he knows for the sake of others he finds he is not able to do it.

9. *Committing the 'terrorism of gossip'. 'It's the sickness of cowardly people who, not having the courage to speak directly, talk behind people's backs.'* This is very common and deeply abusive. People find that personal information disclosed in confidence is leaked out, sometimes through the medium of prayer, or in the context of worship. Lucy (15) experienced exactly that problem when she discovered her confidential story had become common knowledge among her fellow students.

10. **Glorifying one's bosses.** '*It's the sickness of those who court their superiors, hoping for their benevolence. They are victims of careerism and opportunism, they honour people who aren't God.*' Hierarchy and deference are at the root of so many abusive behaviours. Mark's abuse was possible because of the trust and regard he and his mother had for his vicar. Jenny (3), worked in an office where the Heroic Vicar myth was so strong that even though lots of people knew how he treated women no one felt able to challenge him. The extreme grooming and spiritual abuse that happened to Ryan (10) destroyed his and Bethany's relationship. As often happens with families, the whole church community was so groomed that nobody else even noticed that his sermon about Bethany was abusive. The religious language of discipleship was so powerful that Ryan was unable to see what was being done to him. Karen's (5) domestic violence was completely disguised by the deference in which her husband was held.

11. **Being indifferent to others.** '*When, out of jealousy or cunning, one finds joy in seeing another fall rather than helping him up and encouraging him.*' It is hard to overstress how damaging it is to disclose something deeply personal and receive no response from a senior church leader. This behaviour, whatever its cause, is always experienced as contempt. The story of Mark (1) shows just how little senior staff cared about him. Their focus was on making it all go away with as little fuss as possible. This is something survivors say, again and again.

12. **Having a 'funereal face'.** '*In reality, theatrical severity and sterile pessimism are often symptoms of fear and*

78

*insecurity. The apostle must be polite, serene, enthu-
siastic and happy and transmit joy wherever he goes.'*
Working out your pain in someone else's life, consciously or unconsciously, often happens in church life. Muriel (9) suffers bullying by a clergyman who has himself been severely wounded by rejection and bullying
at boarding school. This phenomenon is not limited to
the clergy. Barry (6) has experienced redundancy and a
sense of personal worthlessness, for which he compen-
sates by throwing his weight around in church. Richard Rohr recognises this phenomenon when he says, 'If
you do not transform your pain, you will transmit it in
some way or form to those around you.'

13. **Wanting more.** *'When the apostle tries to
fill an existential emptiness in his heart by
accumulating material goods, not because he
needs them but because he'll feel more secure.'*
This is not just a matter of personal greed. The
Church institutionally often operates its own mean-
spirited material rationing culture. Jennifer (12) needs
psychotherapeutic counselling that may well cost £110
an hour, but the help offered her is capped at £500. It
is very vexing to survivors when an institution of vast
wealth pleads poverty.

14. **Forming closed circles that seek to be stronger
than the whole.** *'This sickness always starts with
good intentions but as time goes by, it enslaves
its members by becoming a cancer that threatens
the harmony of the body and causes so much
bad scandal especially to our younger brothers.'*
There is a strong culture of secrecy in Church which
often kicks in at the least hint of difficulty. It creates
powerful habits of silence. If you do and say nothing,

in the end they'll give up and go away. This is exactly how Desmond, the Cathedral Dean in Mark's story (1), proposes to deal with the matter. Peter (12) the barrister cannot bring himself to break the *omerta* culture of his former schoolmates. An inner circle of boys had been groomed as a cadre of tomorrow's leaders. No matter that Peter didn't even go to church any more. The power over him of that inner circle was still so strong that he was unable to be open and honest about what he knew.

15. ***Seeking worldly profit and showing off.*** *'It's the sickness of those who insatiably try to multiply their powers and to do so are capable of calumny, defamation and discrediting others, even in newspapers and magazines, naturally to show themselves as being more capable than others.'* Mark's abuser, knowing and carrying all that he has done, sails through the preferment processes with flying colours. Father Ian can escape any detailed scrutiny by his senior staff because he is seen as a 'capable mission-minded Catholic', in other words a 'success story'.

The Woes of the Pharisees and the ways they are reflected in churches today show how a complex religious network can become a tight spider's web from which vulnerable individuals cannot escape.

It is this spider's web that survivors encounter when they are in acute pain. They approach the powers-that-be in need of a listening ear, an apology, and a route forward towards healing and restoration. Quite often they have had a deep and life-long commitment of faith. Their church, which had become part of their identity, and on which they have relied, has proved to be a very unsafe place for them. They have been abused in the place they loved by the people they trusted. It is perfectly reasonable to expect a good response when they feel able to tell their story, sometimes years later. It seems obvious to the survivor that the abuse was perpetrated by an individual who was the opposite of the good Christian they expected to encounter in church. They believe the abuser is the anomaly and that the hierarchy will acknowledge this and offer support with some measure of redress. They have every right to expect a loving response simply because that is the essence of the Christian message.

It is therefore a shock of the greatest order to discover that the institution manages to reframe the whole situation so that the survivor becomes the problem. Some survivors prefer to be called 'victims', because they experience the church's response to them as ongoing re-abuse.

They encounter silence and a veiled accusation that what has happened to them is somehow all their fault. They are blamed for being 'damaged'. They are patronised and offered recompense which in no way meets their needs.

They see the Church spending millions on what look like its own vanity projects, like £23.5m for a new library at Lambeth Palace or £27m for new church plants in seaside towns and elsewhere. Meanwhile virtually no provision is offered for their healing or restoration, and the Church's excitement about its new initiatives rubs salt into their wounds.

Theologically, this cuts to the core of our belief. A lawyer asks Jesus, 'What must I do to inherit eternal life?' This is a do or die question. Get it right and you are sorted for eternity, get it wrong and you've got everything wrong. Jesus throws the question back, and the lawyer answers from Scripture:

You shall love the Lord your God with all your heart, with all your soul, and with all your strength and with all your mind, and your neighbour as yourself.

Jesus replies:

You have answered right. Do this and you shall live.

It couldn't be clearer. Loving your neighbour as yourself is the heart of the matter. The lawyer is bright enough to see what a challenge this could be and presses Jesus about exactly whom he should see as his neighbour.

This exchange prompts the parable of the Good Samaritan. Bad as the bandits undoubtedly were, Jesus is not focussed on them. He could have made a new rule that you can never walk from Jerusalem to Jericho alone, or that you must tell your friends about your journey and when you expect to arrive – all good process suggestions. In fact, Jesus is solely interested in the way we respond to need.

A man went down from Jerusalem to Jericho and fell into the hands of bandits; they stripped him, beat him and then made off, leaving him half dead. Now by chance a priest was travelling down the same road, but when he saw the man, he passed by on the other side. In the same way a Levite who came to the place saw him, and passed by on the other side. But a traveller who came on him was moved with compassion when he saw him. He went up to him and bandaged his wounds, pouring oil and wine on them. He then lifted him onto his own mount and took him to an inn and looked after him. Next day, he took out two denarii and handed them to the innkeeper and said, 'Look after him, and on my way back I will make good any extra expense.' 'Which one of these, do you think, proved himself a neighbour to the man who fell into the bandit's hands?' He replied, 'The one who showed mercy towards him.' Jesus said to him, 'Go, and do the same yourself.' (Luke 10. 30-37)

A priest clearly saw the wounded man. He couldn't say 'Oh, I'm so sorry, I didn't see him there.' He looked, he understood and made a conscious decision not to help.

You can imagine the possible thought processes:

'I'm sure someone will be along soon and they'll help him.'

'I'd love to stop but I have a very important service to get to and I don't want to let anyone down.'

'Actually he doesn't look that bad, I expect he'll get over it.'

'I'm not a medic, this looks too tricky. It's one for the experts.'

Indeed someone else did come along. A Levite arrived, and he too clearly saw the man in need. Like the priest he made a conscious decision not to stop and help. This may have been coloured by fear that if the victim were dead contact would make a religious man ritually unclean. Religious duty may thus have compounded wrongdoing. Both men not only walked on by but went to the other side of the road to avoid any contact.

This behaviour, by men who had representative roles within their religion, is behaviour that far too many survivors would recognise. They have written letters that go unanswered for years, they have made phone calls, they have made pleas for help in the media. The deafening silence feels to them like 'passing by on the other side'.

The list of ways to walk past is considerable. It includes hiding behind advice from lawyers and insurers. It includes avoiding internal discomfort from talking about abuse, so that the issue (along with the real person) gets put in the 'too-difficult' box. It can involve a fear of engaging with other people's mental anguish. This gets translated into 'I need to be very careful – these are very damaged people.' This is sometimes true, but hiding behind the fact fails to acknowledge that it was the Church that damaged them in the first place.

Then along came the Samaritan. What he saw was no more and no less than the other two, but he stopped. He put his own plans on hold. He got his hands dirty bandaging the man's wounds. He dipped into his own resources using wine and oil to cleanse and soothe. He put the man on his mount so that he had to walk himself. He had already put himself out, but he chose to go to the nearest inn where he stuck with him until the next day. Finally he gave the innkeeper a sum of money. He could have said, 'Two denarii is what's in the budget for men like this – do your best with it.' But he didn't. What he said was 'Look after him, and on my way back I will make good any extra expense.' In other words his priority was the man's healing and he was prepared to pay what it took to achieve it.

It was all very inconvenient and expensive. It was also clearly the right thing to do.

This is Jesus showing us what good practice looks like. The healing happened because the response was appropriate to that individual. The beaten-up man was seen and recognised as a fellow human being. That moment of choice, to stop or to walk by was crucial, as was the ability to put the needs of others before his own. Finally, the Samaritan tailored the resources to meet the need, not his own budget.

There are survivors who laugh bitterly, from their experience, at the thought the Church could ever be their good Samaritan.

The Church of England often pleads poverty but is seen to be spending millions of pounds on its own mission projects. Can such an institution really be too poor to help those whose lives have been brought to a point of desperation, homelessness and unemployment by what they have suffered within it?

The essence of responding well to the victim was perfectly simple: 'a Samaritan traveler who came on him was moved with compassion when he saw him.'

Therein lies the truth of the matter. The Samaritan helped because he noticed and cared. The priest and the Levite didn't help because, ultimately, they didn't care. They saw a heap of rags on the road, not an equally valuable human being.

It is deeply distressing how often the Church's attitudes and operations fail to acknowledge the humanity of survivors. Some feel airbrushed out of their own stories. This is usually not because of bad will, but inadvertence. Police say a very common category of Road Traffic Collision is what they call a SMIDSY – 'Sorry, mate, I didn't see you.' Theologically, this matters desperately. Jesus does not say the Priest and Levite were especially bad people, but they did fail the basic test for eternal life.

Viewed through the lens of this parable, the matter is perfectly simple. The key to unlocking real change is buried in people's hearts. Too often, the Church buries the matter in policy, more guidelines and appeals to move on. This is usually accompanied by a big fat apology, followed by the statement that things are different now.

The inadequacy of doing this is recognised by Francis X Clooney, Parkman Professor of Divinity and Professor of Comparative Religion at Harvard University:

> It is not enough to look ahead, refining ever stricter rules, if we don't trust those who are to enforce the rules. As Juvenal put it, *Quis custodiet ipsos custodes?* Who watches over those appointed to watch? Even the best of rules won't work, if those on top think that for the good of the Church the sins of its leaders – of themselves – can be overlooked.

The Church's catalogue of failures in this area is no longer an optional issue to be dealt with in some hidden manner. This is a burning platform. Professor Clooney goes on to ask:

> How much damage can 'the sins of the Church' do before 'the faith of the people' makes the whole edifice collapse, for this generation?

3

Doing Likewise

Jesus' command to 'go and do likewise' is the paradigm for responding well when people are hurt in church or anywhere else.

Institutions that do not focus on the victim, focus instead on themselves and their reputations. In 2018 the House of Commons International Development Committee reported on sexual exploitation and abuse in the aid sector and concluded:

> a reactive cyclical approach, driven by concern for reputational management has not, and will never, bring about meaningful change.

So how can we 'do likewise'?

In the following sections, we explore concepts and models that can be turned into a toolbox for understanding and responding to abuse and the culture within which it thrives. We have provided, in Appendix 2 (see p. 214) a diagram showing the ways in which these concepts and models relate to the characters in our tales from the crypt.

First Response, Noticing and Intervention

There is no way of knowing whether the fictional Samaritan was particularly kind or gifted as a paramedic. He did not have to be, because others did that part of the job. His virtue lies in the fact that when he saw something wrong, he did the obvious thing straight away. He took responsibility and helped.

The first response to someone who has been damaged is in many ways the most important. If a paramedic fails to keep you alive until you reach the hospital, you're dead. It really doesn't matter how skilled the team waiting for you there is. If they get you to A & E alive, the quality of first response does much to shape a victim's whole experience of care.

Therefore doing nothing should never be an option. It doesn't matter what was intended or why. Even if the person who does nothing is a senior figure with a big Too-Difficult box, the victim will inevitably experience their silence as contempt. Those who fail to respond adequately are judged on how their acts came over to the victim, not their good intentions. Anyone in distress needs to know they are being taken seriously by someone who cares, even though it may initially be possible to offer little more than a listening ear.

The Church will find it difficult to establish a fruitful healing relationship with anyone if it has failed to respond to them adequately on first contact. 'I am shocked to hear about your experience and will try and establish how I can help; I will get back to you in a fortnight' is a much better first response than, 'I will pray for you at this testing time while someone else (unspecified) responds.' If the next thing the victim experiences is a thick wall of silence, intended or unintended, their suffering is compounded. Silence soon becomes deafening to someone anxiously awaiting a response.

No Rotten Apples

Churches very often describe their abusers as 'Rotten Apples in the Barrel'. All institutions find this hypothesis useful. It is appealing for many reasons. It fixes guilt clearly by throwing a *cordon sanitaire* around the abuser. It enables scapegoating. It evades the hard question of what abuse reveals about the institutional system within which it occurred. It heads off any demand for change that may arise from it. Churches have often moved their rotten apples around behind the scenes, hoping this will minimise embarrassment and solve the problem.

Military boards of inquiry, classically, 'Shoot the Sergeant'. Throwing the offender under the bus enables everyone else to step away, and evade institutional responsibility. It smacks of the way the priest and Levite behaved, not the good Samaritan.

The 'Rotten Apple in the Barrel' model is not only evasive, it cannot explain what has actually happened. Abuse of any kind occurs in a social context. Every abusive deed is likely to involve at least three people – the abuser, the abusee, and (usually) several people groomed by the abuser to enable them to gain access and cover up afterwards.

So, for example, the story of Anna the pregnant teenager (2) could be understood in terms of a single predator and his victim. That, however, would not be the whole truth. Suzy, the friend who took her along to choir in the first place, played a vital role, albeit unwittingly. When Vince, the Curate, excluded her from the second youth group planning meeting, she could have reacted more strongly. Understandably she didn't, not wanting, perhaps, to appear jealous. As a result Anna found herself alone with Vince in what she had assumed would be a group meeting. Vince prevented her from feeling she could tell anyone about what was going on by making it 'our little secret'. Abuse always involves rings within rings. Abusers groom victims and the networks around them by establishing interlocking circles of unwitting complicity.

A skilled perpetrator will camouflage what they do in the regular life of the church. They will game its system, including its deep structures, to gain access and cover up afterwards. It follows that serious attention needs to be paid to the social context of abuse. To spot a rotten apple, we need to understand everything that is going on in the barrel. The key to safety is that an anomaly looks like an anomaly. Only then can it be treated as such and responded to appropriately.

Opening up closed systems

Religions involve universal claims about truth and life. They usually have formal or informal hierarchies to which deference is due. They create their own worlds. They enter people's bloodstreams and become assumptions about reality. The more intense and immersive this process is for any individual, the more danger they are in of abuse. To put it crudely, the more Kool-Aid you drink, the more danger there is of being poisoned.

Faith touches every aspect of religious people's lives. It engages deep convictions and emotions. It gives rise to a distinctive sense of identity far more powerful, for good or for evil, than is often appreciated. Every religion needs sufficient organisation to maintain its coherence, survive and propagate itself. This means it will tend to operate as a more or less closed system.

Pat Baranowski experienced inappropriate physical abuse from her pastor at Willow Creek, a US nondenominational Evangelical megachurch. Her faith made it impossible to complain for many years.

> I really did not want to hurt the church ... I felt like if this was exposed, this fantastic place would blow up, and I loved the church. I loved the people there. I loved the family. I didn't want to hurt anybody. And I was ashamed.

Abuse like this happens in all kinds of churches, including more traditional ones. When Jenny (3) became uncomfortable with her boss Mike's behaviour, her colleague Fiona warned her off. She knew all about Mike's poor track record, but the way in which churchwardens had handled previous allegations, by keeping everything in house, dampened her response. Abuse was thus normalised within the system, and it became impossible for Jenny to break out of it.

Richard Scorer, a lawyer who has acted for many English abuse survivors, had this to say of one prominent Anglican charismatic abuser:

> What is now very clear is that, in the Church of England, Peter Ball found the perfect cover for his offending. If a charlatan with an insatiable appetite for abuse wanted to secure a continuous supply of vulnerable young victims, there was no better way of achieving this than by founding a religious order not subject to any external supervision and by making his victims' participation in the abuse a religious duty obligated by their oath of absolute obedience. Not for the first time, theology and religious ritual provided the ideal mask for abuse with the evil of what Peter Ball did being compounded by his nauseating claim that the abuse was spiritually uplifting. Most of all, however, Peter Ball found in his fellow bishops in the Church of England the perfect accomplices, prepared to turn a blind eye to his abuse over many decades, to collude in the lie that the abuse of Neil Todd was an uncharacteristic aberration, to cast doubt on his guilt, to smear his victims and to rehabilitate him.

Religious communities shape the lives of those within them. Therefore, as one blogger observed about Pat Baranowski's Willow Creek experience:

> organised religion does two thirds of the work of grooming.

One might feel that the only way to ensure personal safety is to steer clear of all religion. Abuse, however, occurs in all social organisations.

Religion doesn't have to be abusive, in and of itself. Millions of people find meaning, social solidarity and personal nourishment in church membership. Their urge to belong and find meaning in life, however, makes them vulnerable.

The whole church community has to take responsibility for its own safety. Churches can only be safe if everybody at every level within them exercises vigilance, with a positive duty of care towards one another. Only in this way can the barrel become a healthy microclimate, within which rotten apples cannot thrive.

Making religion safer

How can we ensure religious life is safe? What amber warning lights could we recognise for potentially dangerous anomalies?

The twentieth-century psychiatrist Robert Jay Lifton studied the experience of servicemen captured in the Korean War along with mainland Chinese people who had suffered psychological abuse during Chairman Mao's cultural revolution. He analysed the experience of fifteen Chinese escapees and twenty five Westerners and wrote up his research in 1961 as *Thought Reform and the Psychology of Totalism: A Study of 'brainwashing' in China*.

The people he studied were not trapped in religious cults. His analysis, however, can help us understand all types of controlling behaviour, including those experienced in religious institutions.

Lifton identified eight criteria for what he termed 'thought reform'. These can be used to identify abusive patterns and behaviours, especially in closed subgroups. They reflect almost uncannily aspects of the experience of many people in our fifteen tales from the Crypt. Lifton's original diagnosis was based on study of non-religious abuse. His conclusions cannot therefore be viewed as a secular attack on religion.

1 **Milieu Control**

Information and communication are carefully controlled within the environment around the abusee. Ultimately, they may internalise what is communicated and how, building up an identity that isolates them from society at large, and creates a circle within which norms are different, and the incredible becomes acceptable. The scope of dogma is total, both by taking in the largest questions of life and existence, and by staying in touch in the long term, to control and achieve its larger ends.

A commonly experienced feature of all kinds of abuse is corralling victims, individually or as a group, into a space within which abuse can happen. This means isolating the victim so that it is harder for them to whistleblow. There are many ways of doing this. Very many sex abuses in schools involve particular elite groups, like sports teams or choirs. Abusers often tell their victims like Anna (2) to 'let this be our little secret'. Rufus (10) was more sophisticated. He recruited Ryan into a special leadership cadre, in order to isolate him from Bethany. As a result his strong relationship with his partner, far from protecting him, was used against him. Rufus denounced her from the pulpit so that for Ryan she became a siren voice, tempting him away from the elite group that was becoming his alternative reality.

C. S. Lewis presented a memorial lecture at King's College London in 1944 called 'the inner ring.' He observed the way in which vulnerable young people like his Oxford students, become aware as they grow up of various elite circles.

> I believe that in all men's lives at certain periods, and in many men's lives at all periods between infancy and extreme old age, one of the most dominant elements is

the desire to be inside the 'ring' and the terror of being left outside.

If you ask many abuse survivors why they ever put themselves in what turned out to be harm's way, this motivation figures highly. They have usually been part of an isolation group like the special boys selected by the games master for extra coaching, or by the vicar for the altar party. The group can have only one member, like the promising young musician to whom the organist will give special organ lessons, or the enthusiastic young person who will help relaunch the youth group. When Anna (2) began to see herself as the latter, she was hooked.

Even a marriage can become an inner ring, with an exclusive claim to loyalty and deference. Karen (5), abused clergy wife, is trapped in a place where it is impossible for her to disclose her husband David's violence against her. Her religious beliefs about marriage and gender roles trap her.

She accidentally discloses to Angela the churchwarden who herself has a considerable investment in pastors having exemplary family lives. Thus Angela's beliefs compound Karen's isolation. This mechanism is so powerful that even though Karen has told Angela, she goes on to ask her to cover up, and Angela actually agrees, albeit with regret. She cannot bring herself to do the right thing. She is also disabled by the power of the inner ring.

Boarding school survivors carry a special vulnerability, described by psychotherapists like Nick Duffell and Joy Schaverien. Jonty (9), the son of missionaries, finds himself displaced from the security of a close family, isolated, and put into the care of people who do not love him. He blanks out his feelings as a survival strategy. This enables him to get by in the cruel and unjust environment of his school. He has always believed God was his heavenly father, and hopes that, as the Bible puts it, 'when my father and my mother forsake me, the Lord taketh me up'. Sadly the survival mechanism that he developed to protect himself as an eight-year-old eventually turns him into a bullying prefect like the others. More disturbingly, it is still an essential part of his operating system thirty years later. Without realising it, the abused prep school boy becomes an abusive vicar.

This same kind of vulnerability can be seen in Peter (4), who joins an elite camp for boys at top schools. This turns out to be a whole nested set of inner rings, led by a charismatic leader. Many years later, another camper's revelations of abuse triggers a need to speak out and support his friend from camp but his fear of being rejected by the tribe produces an internalised loyalty that makes it impossible for him to do so.

The effect on abusees of being in one or more inner rings is to isolate them, increasing their vulnerability. The same rings provide privileged access for their abusers. They also reinforce the abuser's ability to get away with it and cover up. Anomalies cease to look like anomalies, even to victims, their families and friends. This creates and sustains a totalising form of 'milieu control'.

2   Mystical Manipulation

Experiences are planned and orchestrated by the group or its leaders to demonstrate something beyond earthly authority, their capacity to develop members spiritually, or some x-factor that sets the leader and group apart from the rest of humanity. This often involves a particular in-group way of interpreting Scripture, or the group's history. Coincidences and happenstances are turned into omens, prophecies, or other buttresses to sustain the plausibility structure of the group.

Religious groups often claim they develop people spiritually, and possess special truth that sets members over and above the rest of humanity. Such mystical manipulation is something of an occupational hazard in religion, especially for groups that are particularly world-denying. Scriptures are quarried for suitable soundbites to reinforce the authority of the group and its leaders over their followers. The whole compelling package is self-sustaining. Potential abusees internalise this process, which is regularly reinforced by shared rituals. It becomes their self-identity as well as the lens through which they see the outside world.

This danger does not negate other-worldly authority *per se*. It does, however, call for heightened vigilance when it is claimed and acknowledged. The larger and more totalising the claim, the more self-critically and carefully it needs to be treated.

A self-contained group tends to produce its own culture of self-protecting secrecy. Intensely religious circles, like Mark's serving team (1) or Peter's Evangelical camps (4) are places where mystical manipulation is most likely to occur. Daylight disinfects. Groups with less exalted claims should be more willing to allow outsiders to monitor their activities.

Forms of mystical manipulation occur in almost all Church abuse. It figures, albeit implicitly, in stories like Jenny's in the parish office (3), Muriel's as a volunteer with a bullying vicar (9), Lucy's vulnerability as an ordinand (15), Geoff's disempowerment as a junior priest (7), even Karen's as a clergy wife (5).

Evidence of it, in any form, is a major danger signal.

3   **Demand for Purity**

The world is viewed in black and white. Members are made aware of the gap between the group and the world, and exhorted to conform to group ideology. Nothing but the best is good enough. Guilt and shame are powerful weapons for the abuser, the former to internalise silence and the latter to quell any tendency to whistleblow.

A flat two dimensional view of the world figures more obviously in some religious contexts than others. Binary messages that say 'I am right and they are wrong' appeal to people who like simple answers to life's questions, especially young people whose brains and critical faculties are still growing.

This kind of logic offers abusers great potential. To succeed, an abuser has to neutralise the critical sense of their abusees and friends. Strong world-denying dogma is an excellent hook for those who are insecure, with its own magnetic romantic appeal. It grows into a powerful framework within which people increasingly suspend disbelief. The more greyscale there is in group members' minds, the more room for doubt and questioning. High walls over and against the rest of the world inhibit critical thinking. Any external challenge can be framed as an attack on the group, and any self-questioning as betrayal.

Moral and theological absolutism is a highly effective seedbed for abuse. This phenomenon is by no means confined to notorious US Fundamentalist preachers. Bishop Peter Ball had his own warped Catholic perspective. He secured fulsome support from people who should have known better. They saw him as a charismatic holy man, standing alone against the secular world, winning young people back for Christ.

Guilt and shame are powerful human drivers.

They figure more highly in some theologies than others. There is a scale from world-affirming to world-denying. It doesn't help that the New Testament uses the word 'world' in various ways. Sometimes it is negative in an almost dualistic way – 'friendship with the world is enmity with God'. Sometimes, however, it is far more positive about the world – 'God so loved the world'. If one of these perspectives predominates in an unhealthy way, a total negativity may develop about the real world. This can easily shield abusers from outside scrutiny.

Purists present personal sin in a lurid way. They then invite their followers to see themselves as worthless and confess their faults so that they can be offered salvation through a transactional model of atonement. This was what Peter's Public Schoolboy camps (4) did. The leaders' teaching was loaded with specific guilt triggers around sexual sins that are almost universal behaviours among schoolboys. In this way the group and its leader used a demand for purity to establish and maintain their power.

4 Confession
The group has its own code of behaviour, based on that of wider society but more specific. Totalising groups lay a very strong stress on moral conformity. Confession to a personal mentor enforces the code, or sometimes public confession in a group context. There is no confidentiality from the leaders. The whole range of members' lives, doings and misdoings are material for the leaders to maintain control.

If knowledge is power, the flow of information in abusive relationships has to be one-sided. The abuser needs to establish a relationship in which the abused are unable to assert their will against the way they are being treated. Lip service is usually paid to the idea 'we're all sinners,' but the abuser will always know more about the abusee than vice versa. This is an essential thread in the spider's web by which the victim is trapped.

Abusers use personal information to establish and maintain control. Lucy (15) discovered that information she believed to be confidential really wasn't. The Diocesan Director of Ordinands leaked it, and soon enough the story spread through a network of people who seemed to think others needed to know. Soon enough it was all around the college.

Scriptures that call for Christians to confess their sins to one another (James 5:16), can be used to break down natural reticence about sharing personal information. The act of confession, whether in a Maoist show trial, a Bishop Peter Ball monastic 'scheme', or a Public School Evangelical Camp, seals the deal and binds the victim into their own abuse.

A most basic expression of human dignity is privacy. Sensitive personal information is turned over to the group or its leader with a high likelihood that the resulting vulnerability will be exploited. Thus the victim becomes permanently dependent on those who hold power over them.

In this way Lucy the ordinand (15) discovers that an incident that caused her pain came back to bite her from an unexpected direction. Once her information is out there, she has lost control over it.

This happens in informal settings, too. Norman (14) did not want the prayer ministry team at St Peter's to pray for his sexuality to be healed but they did it anyway. It is not unknown for people to reveal to a prayer group that they are gay, and then be shunned by the Church and banned from ministry, home group, or even communion. An incident was reported to the Oxford Diocesan Synod in June 2018 of a person being removed from a coffee rota because they had said they were gay.

All abuse is ultimately abuse of power. Abusive confession differs in two ways from the means laid down in the Book of Common Prayer to relieve troubled conscience.

First, confession must be voluntary. The conventional Anglo-Catholic understanding of confession has been 'all may, none must, some should.' There is a world of difference between voluntarily giving personal information to someone you trust and being expected to confess, perhaps as the price of remaining a member of the group or simply as 'something we all do'.

Second, if someone confesses their sins within the highly structured discipline of the Sacrament of Reconciliation the information should remain private in all but the most extreme circumstances. The norm for confessors has been 'in one ear and out the other'. The seal cannot be absolute in all circumstances or the Sacrament becomes what the Bible calls 'a cloak of maliciousness.' Disclosure of a serious crime likely to put others in danger, past or future, needs to be responsibly handled.

There has been much debate around the seal of the confessional and its potential to cover up abuse. There have to be circumstances under which the rights of the abusee are placed before those of the abuser, and disclosure of crime is reported.

Within the more informal disciplines of less Catholic groups there is as great, if not greater, need for caution. There should be clear understanding all round why someone is giving information, and how it will be used. Any contract of confidentiality has to be negotiated freely, not assumed or imposed. Muddle about confidentiality, or any other aspect of how information is used, has to be a significant danger signal.

5 Sacred Science

The group has a strong dogmatic core that is non-negotiable. Any dispute or questioning is seen as subversive. There is no truth outside the totalising group, whose leader is held to be above criticism.

People who study early Christianity sometimes expect to discover a tightly-disciplined church, on message. What they find is the exact opposite. Early Christians argued passionately about various subjects, often basic to the faith. Could an uncircumcised person be baptised? And once baptised, could a Christian who sinned be restored? If so how? St Paul faced down St Peter, calling him a hypocrite and challenging him to repent. This was not unusual behaviour in the early church. It took many years for norms to evolve clearly. Early Christians were open about dogma, unlike the gnostic cults of the ancient world with their exclusive truth claims and secret rituals.

Cults thrive on simplification and exclusivity. Non-members see clearly that contradictory claims cannot all be right at once. The totalising power of a cult closes off such thinking. It frames the horizon of all experience in terms of dogma. An effectively infallible leader and trusted lieutenants form and police cult members, top-down.

Jason (8) uses sacred science to cover his tracks. He has been drinking too much, and knows he has been reported for it. He tries to neutralise complaints and enlist followers by preaching a sermon accusing his enemies of blaspheming against the Holy Spirit. Jason skilfully turns himself from a drunk into a persecuted martyr. The bottle becomes a theological issue. He can then go home and pour himself another drink secure in the knowledge that what some see as his problem is in fact their fault.

The Church articulates its core beliefs carefully and symbolically using creeds. When dogma that goes beyond them is asserted in absolute terms this has to be a matter of concern, an amber light.

6   Loaded Language

The group has its own language to define who is in and who is out. Its linguistic markers usually take the form of ordinary words and phrases laden with particular meaning for members of the in-group. The group has its own banter but also uses what Lifton calls 'thought-terminating clichés.' These are taglines or soundbites that mark the limit of permitted thought. This harnesses language to discourage dissent and promote group-think.

Nursery teachers say, 'Language defines my world'. This remains largely the case as we grow up. Language articulates the lines along which thinking and logic run. All human groups, from Morris Dancers to Freemasons develop their own banter and jargon. This is an important tool to gather members and embed them within the group.

Groups invest words and phrases with extra meaning of their own when they use them to identify insiders and outsiders. When Mrs Thatcher called a subsection of her political rivals within the Conservative party 'Wets' everybody knew what to make of them, and the fact they were not 'one of us'.

Totalising groups use language for the particular purpose of defining the in-group and securing party discipline. Claims to be 'orthodox' are charged with the implication that everybody else is 'heterodox' and therefore must not be taken as seriously as cult members. Trigger words and pixie phrases become passwords to identify friends and foes alike.

Religious arguments often end in thought terminating clichés. For example, there are several thousand commentaries and articles offering diverse interpretations of LGBT+ 'clobber texts' in the Bible. Christians read them in good faith in various ways. Yet a common ending to social media spats on the subject is a thought-terminating cliché, 'The Bible clearly teaches'. Whatever the rights and wrongs of the matter itself, the Bible plainly does no such thing.

Totalising language has sometimes been applied to joining a group, for example, where religious conversion has been described as 'coming through' – terminology that sounds more gnostic than Christian. It carries with it a whole hinterland of elitist theological assumptions.

Rufus (10) uses language powerfully to establish his credibility. When he is telling his PCC about the conference he has attended he declares that God has given him a 'Numbers 11 Vision' as though that is all there is to say on the matter. When Ivy the verger challenges this simple thought terminating cliché, he slaps her down as ignorant. His proposal for Ryan to join what he calls his 'A-Team' is almost entirely couched in absolutist clichés that flatter Ryan whilst holding out before him the golden promise that he could join an inner circle.

Controlling people through the use of loaded language that is inaccessible to outsiders must be an amber light.

7 Doctrine over Person

Members' personal stories are used to buttress the group's ideology. Experiences that confirm the rightness of it all become testimony to be shared as part of its story. Experiences that call into question any aspect of core dogma, or the leaders' authority, are strenuously denied or reinterpreted.

There are two ways of doing theology.

One starts from human experience – 'Inductive' to use the technical term. 'The World is all that is the case' (Wittgenstein). Any doctrine flows from this basic fact. Truth is contingent and emergent. Theology describes people's aggregated experience of God. Not all experience is equally valid or valuable, but inductive theologians draw their conclusions from human knowledge and experience.

A good example of this is Jesus' way of answering the lawyer's question: 'Is it lawful to heal on the sabbath?' (Matthew 12:10-12). He might have launched into a learned exposition of the concept of 'Sabbath' and drawn out its implications. Instead he asked his hearers 'if one of you has a sheep that falls into a ditch on the Sabbath, what do you do?' A very small amount of imagination establishes that healing someone is more important to God than rescuing a sheep, *et voilà*. That's the answer.

The opposite way of doing theology is to start with dogma – the 'Deductive' method. It works out life's 'ises' from its 'oughts'. Starting from first principles, it interprets real life experience in their terms.

An example of this way of approaching theology is Jesus' method in the parable of the Good Samaritan along with its contextual dialogue. The lawyer asks Jesus his question, 'what is the greatest commandment?' Jesus answers the question in its own terms, referring the lawyer to standard texts. The lawyer comes back with a technical request for a ruling that will define the concept of 'neighbour'. Jesus blows the lid off the whole legal argument by contextualising it. He invites the lawyer to apply the law in a way which undermines his original attempt 'to justify himself' with an inductive question 'Who, then, was neighbour to the man who fell among robbers?'

The ethicist Carol Gilligan has suggested there is a gendered aspect to inductive and deductive reasoning.

Men and women follow different voices. Men tend to organize social relationships in a hierarchical order and subscribe to a morality of rights. Females value interpersonal connectedness, care, sensitivity, and responsibility to people ... However, she does not claim that one system is better; both are equally valid. Only by integrating these complementary male (justice) and female (care) orientations will we be able to realize our full human potential in moral development.

In the Gospels, Jesus used both inductive and deductive approaches depending on the context. The lawyer got a lawyer's answer, and the farmer a farmer's.

Totalising cults are about control. Thus, they almost always do their theology deductively. Principles matter more than people. Mao's cultural revolutionaries were none too worried about their enemies' feelings and experiences, but spent hours bickering about the dogma in the Little Red Book.

Religious custom as well as theology can also inhibit empathetic responses. Dan and Yvette (13) are shown callous indifference. The principle that gravestones should only use specific colours has no moral or theological basis. Alison, the vicar, is required to impose the Chancellor's taste with a rod of iron on a vulnerable grieving family. Fortunately Alison and John the curate have the decency and humanity to put human needs before a regulation that is based on no more than the personal aesthetic of a Church official. Jesus said: 'The Sabbath was made for people, not people for the Sabbath.' Any pastoral imposition that asserts the opposite should be treated with great suspicion – another amber light.

8 Dispensing of Existence
Pure group leadership can decide who can be considered to exist and who cannot. In the Korean War this could be a simple matter of life and death. In religious cults outsiders are often seen as 'unsaved'. Any critique from the outside is suppressed or, if it cannot be ignored, made to strengthen a sense of 'Here's to us, who's like us?' Any attempt to influence the group must be filtered through the group leaders. Any member who dares to try and leave is ostracised.

The more a group is behaving like a cult, the less its pattern of relationships will look like a net of connected equals, and the more like a hub and spokes. Communication between the members of a pure cult goes through the leaders or their lieutenants, who monitor everything that goes on among the members. Some organisations like the Church of Scientology, appear to devote enormous energy to this.

The ultimate sanction a group has is to throw dissidents out. In a religious cult this will almost always involve spiritual sanctions and, with extreme offences, relegation to the ranks of the unsaved – withholding eternal life. The lines dividing saints from apostates have to be hard and clear. Tales of their apostasy must be told in a way that will discourage other members from following suit.

Even groups who do not actually kill people, fired

by religious passion, can come to believe they have a
right to behave as though they could. Stephen Mattson
describes some Moody Bible Institute students' reaction
to the 9/11 atrocity, and the way this reinforced their
conviction of their own righteousness. They drew the
outline of a Muslim terrorist on a mattress and threw
knives at it:

> Soon long lines of Bible students were eagerly awaiting
> their chance. What became known as the 'anti-terrorist
> camp' quickly became a popular attraction for guys on
> campus. Throwing knives requires a certain amount of
> skill and a lot of practice. Being college students with
> nothing better to do, we became quite good at it. We
> threw, we sliced, and we stabbed. Eventually it turned
> into a game of 'Who can make the knife stick into
> the terrorist from the farthest away?' With a morbid
> passion inspired by hate, patriotism, and fear, we
> unleashed violence upon this unnamed Islamic enemy
> and defended our country – God's country – from evil
> forces. The anti-terrorist camp lasted for days. Every
> morning we'd pretend to torture and kill hundreds of
> Muslim terrorists. Then we'd go to our classes and learn
> about God. Later in the day we might even walk the
> streets of Chicago and evangelize to strangers, telling
> them about the wonderful love of Jesus. So there I was:
> a bloodlusting, hate-filled, revenge-seeking Christian.
> But that's how nearly everyone I knew was. I remember
> how I felt during that time: confident, holy, righteous,
> and assured that everything I believed in was right.

Wise Christian leaders, however radical or conservative
their convictions may be, leave judging to God. Leaders
who can't do this may indulge in excommunication or
badmouthing potential dissidents, in the way Bethany

found herself all but named from the pulpit, deemed a distraction to her boyfriend Ryan (10).

When abuse survivors are blanked by Church officials, it feels as if their whole existence is being called into question. For people who have often already lost much, losing their voice is unbearable. Twitter may not be the safest or most expressive environment within which to speak, but at least someone is listening and will react.

It is no wonder that blanking, intentional or not, evokes strong passions among survivors. This, and any other reaction to abuse that seems to call into question survivors' right to exist, is cruel and dangerous. Any evidence of behaviour or attitudes that do this should be treated as a glaring amber light.

4

How do they get away with it?

The key to all safeguarding is noticing an anomaly for what it is and responding. What should we be looking out for, how do we understand what we've seen, and how can we actually do anything about it? What exactly are we responding to? When should an amber light turn red? Who was involved, and how? What routes led into and out of danger?

The simplest response to crime and incompetence is the hallowed 'bloody fool theory'. This deposits all the blame on an individual or very small number of individuals. It has the virtue of simplicity. Identify the Bloody Fool and punish them – what is sometimes called 'shoot the sergeant'.

This theory can only explain any crime or abuse in the most superficial way. Sergeants work within systems, and we cannot establish safe culture without securing systems against rogue individuals.

Take a famous military near-disaster involving nuclear weapons. On 18 September 1980 in Arkansas a maintenance crew member accidentally dropped a socket wrench into the well of a silo containing a Titan V missile. It bounced off the bottom, punctured the stage 2 fuel tank and started a leak that threatened to collapse the missile. This accident set off a chain of events that almost culminated in a thermonuclear explosion more powerful than all the bombs, including atom bombs, dropped in the Second World War.

The Damascus Titan Missile Explosion could simply

be seen as a maintenance man's bad day at the office. Only by going further than that and asking radical systemic questions about how such a thing was possible, could the chances of a future similar catastrophe be reduced.

Context, then is everything. To make the Church the safe place it professes to be, we need a more rigorous model of abuse than rotten apples in the barrel or the 'Bloody Fool' theory. It calls for a systemic model. This has to be simple enough to be applied to complex situations by anyone who notices an anomaly and cares enough to want to do something about it.

Understanding abuse
Two simple questions can be asked about any abuse:

1   'How did the abuser secure access to the abusee and cover their tracks afterwards?'

2   'Why did they get away with it?'

The answers to these questions reveal what could be termed its Vector and Signature. The Vector describes the human dynamics of the abuse, and the Signature its character.

Vector
Abuse is never a single act out of the blue. We cannot understand any abuse without recognising that it is the culmination of a developing scenario. To scope what is going on we have to identify the elements of the grooming process that exploited a vulnerability. What was the setup? What held the victim in a dangerous place, and how was a getaway accomplished, and tracks covered?

Plotting the Vector usually reveals a pattern that repeats itself. Victims of domestic violence often tolerate repeated cycles of behaviour. One powerful aid for plotting the vector of domestic violence is the Duluth Power Wheel (Appendix 3). The human reality is simple – a drunken boyfriend beats up his victim every weekend, then apologises profusely with flowers or chocolates. Hope triumphs over experience again and again. Especially when the victim loves her abuser, this brings a 'killer hope,' always disappointed, that the most recent act of violence will be the last, and his apology really will lead to change.

All abuse rests on an assertion of power over someone weaker. Perpetrators characteristically refuse to take responsibility for their use of power. Sometimes they even deny they have any power. Having abused an employee or parishioner, as Mike (3) abused Jenny they describe what ensued as mutual. They neatly sidestep the imbalance of power inherent in the working relationship.

This does not mean that relationships can only be mutual between people on the same rung of the career ladder, but positional inequality is a serious issue that must be negotiated carefully between partners with equal voices before there can be a genuinely mutual relationship. Where there is gross inequality, especially where one party is in no position to give or withhold consent, mutuality is impossible. This is yet another reason why child sex abuse is always wrong.

Plotting the vector of an abusive incident begins by identifying all the people involved.

Mark's story (1), for example, could be said to have begun when he was wheeled up the vicarage path for his mother to arrange his baptism. Pauline is no more responsible directly for what subsequently happened with Father Ian than Father Archie. Her reluctance to believe Mark when he tries to whistleblow later arises partly, however, from her trust for the Church and its priests, kindled when she met Father Archie. Similarly the vicar's prophetic word at the christening, like Stanley the Head

Server's ethical relationship with Mark, do not carry direct responsibility for Father Ian's subsequent abuse. They are, however, elements in the story without which it cannot be understood.

The Church has become for Mark an environment of stability and meaning. It has always been part of his life, and he senses his value, personally and spiritually, within it. His status as a server folds him seamlessly into the institution. He finds nourishment within it, and invests great trust in its leaders, especially his priest. An invitation for extra server training at the vicarage makes him feel special, and raises no apprehension. Even when Father Ian asks him to do things he has never done before and does not want to do, he is in no position to say no.

Mark is now trapped in a situation beyond his control or understanding, with no means of escape. Those elements in his religious commitment that might have given him the strength to whistleblow are almost certainly closed off by the way he perceives his priest as an authority figure. The Church that enfolds him traps him in a dangerous place. He may feel that what happens to him at the vicarage is wrong but how can it be when the priest who leads his confession and gives him absolution is the perpetrator?

None of the incidental characters along the vector that led Mark into abuse can be held responsible for what ensued, until Father Ian came on the scene.

The same cannot be said of the Church's response afterwards. The possibility of abuse, once raised creates a responsibility to respond. When this is done badly, a whole new dimension is added to the original crime.

The Church hierarchy beyond the parish compounds Mark's abuse. None of them consciously wishes him harm. The diocese's initial response is a mixture of bumbling complacency, sloppy communication and fudge. They may wish to excuse themselves by saying that their failures were benign blunders, not malign. From the survivor's perspective, they might as well have been, given the devastating effect they had on Mark's life.

How can senior Church figures, who intend so little harm, do so much?

Part of the answer is that like Mark and Father Ian, they are deeply inculturated in the Church. People who prosper in any institution, the kind of people who end up as senior ecclesiastics, are very likely to define and value themselves almost entirely in terms of that Institution. They have drunk the Kool-Aid. They will tend to frame any evidence of possible institutional failure as a threat. Unless they take very active steps to control such feelings, they cannot respond well to the needs of a survivor they may easily wish did not exist. They will see their highest duty as being to protect the Church's reputation.

Why was Mark so enraged when the institution invested more of itself in Father Ian by making him a bishop? The impact of the original abuse partially explains it, but everything is compounded because Mark's abuser has been rewarded by the Church which should have protected him. Everybody involved would protest their good intentions towards him, but what matters is not what they intended, but what they did, or did not do.

Institutional pen pushers often assume the safest course of action is inaction. At least then they can't get into trouble for anything they have done. This tactic can succeed with the internal business of a complex bureaucracy. When, however, doing nothing is experienced as active contempt, it will radically compound the abuse that has already been suffered.

A large dispersed and complex organisation like the Church of England has many dark corners in which things can be parked and forgotten. Its servants easily fail to see the human being by the roadside. No wonder the Church responded to Mark by addressing its own need, not his. Responsibility has effectively been evaded. No wonder, either, that Mark explodes with anger when the Church goes on to appoint Ian as a bishop.

Failure to respond properly has also left Father Ian free to continue offending. It posed a real danger to the public, as well as a risk of Mark self-harming in some way. This was far more than a bureaucratic glitch. The Church had elaborate and much-trumpeted safeguarding policies. What was lacking was something one might hope any of the senior churchmen involved should have seen as their primary duty – the imagination to notice, acknowledge and help the victim in the way the Good Samaritan did.

Signature

Plotting the Vector sets the abusee's experience in context. It raises the question of what they were doing there in the first place, and why they found themselves at risk. To engage with the question 'why?' as well as the question 'what?', we need to describe the particular and distinctive characteristics of the abuse, its signature.

Another way of seeing abuse in church is as a failure in the Church's pastoral care system. A classic model for understanding system failure, from surgical mistakes to industrial accidents, is the 'Swiss Cheese' model developed by Professor James Reason.

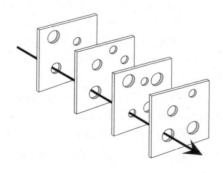

The loss is plotted as a trajectory through various protective layers, any one of which could normally have been expected to prevent harm. In order to understand the system failure, it is necessary to describe why the layers lined up, like levers in a lock, and allowed harm to occur. In terms of the model proposed here, the line is the Vector. The placing of the holes is the Signature.

The Vector began with a cast list. Everyone involved has to be considered in relation to each other, as clearly and dispassionately as possible. This makes it possible to discern how any particular part of the Church system might have functioned better to prevent rather than allow harm.

Mark's abuse happened in an Anglo-Catholic urban church. This had its own particular concepts of God, family, authority, morality, wonder, tradition, shame and guilt. He was a much loved child from a caring home. His parents always wanted to protect him. His parish church should have been a place of safety – a structured community within which any danger should have been identified and dealt with. Within the parish the servers' team was a sub-community ably led by Stanley. The parish priest was, on paper, a professional trained pastor. If the red line made it through all of these holes, the parish church was part of a diocese overseen by archdeacon and bishop, with a rural dean and colleagues, any of whom, setting the good shepherd always before them, would have wanted to deter abuse. They certainly should have made things better, not worse after it was reported. Failing all else, the ten commandments and the law of love should have secured Mark's safety.

Yet somehow this whole system failed. Mark was abused by his priest, and that threw everything around him into reverse, turning its protective aspects into instruments of abuse, a cage in which he was trapped. Anita tried to do the sensible and loving thing, but was powerless in the face of the Church's instinct for self-preservation and its overriding need to save face.

Thus the normal priest's role was inverted. Father Ian ceased to be a shepherd and became a wolf in sheep's clothing. The serving team became a flypaper on which Mark was trapped. His parents were sufficiently in thrall to a charismatic young clergyman to disbelieve their son. They were unable or unwilling to see beyond the priest's institutional role in which they trusted. Father Ian's superiors were reluctant to believe him capable of abuse. Their sloppy and offhand way of communicating with each other and with Mark flew in the face of their official duties. It covered up, and bred complacency about their own performance in role.

The critical point is that at every point higher authorities were more interested in their institution and its reputation than they were in Mark. Thus the victim was transformed in their minds into a threat. Eventually, when the story ended up in the press, their bungling had provoked exactly the crisis they feared most. In response they closed ranks, made excuses, and attempted to ride out the storm. By now Mark was showing signs of extreme trauma, like the breakdown of his marriage. At the end of his reabuse he was far more injured and ignored than ever.

Each abusive act has its own distinctive Signature. One extreme example lay unexposed for many years but is now in the public domain. Almost a hundred boys in the UK and Africa are said to have been violently abused by the John Smyth QC, Chair of the Iwerne Trust, in the 1980s and 1990s.

The Vector was simple. Smyth chaired a trust that ran holiday camps for boys at leading public schools. He was well known for his Conservative ethical views. He was barrister for Mary Whitehouse, the mid-century morality campaigner. He had, however, a strange sexual taste for violently beating naked boys. The camps gave access, and combined with his proximity to Winchester College, its Evangelical Christian Forum provided a supply of boys. In 1981 stories began to emerge of what he was doing. He was banned from the College, but subsequently enabled to continue his abuse in Zimbabwe by powerful supporters in Canada and the UK. One boy, Guide Nyachuru, died. UK police were not involved until many years later. Smyth died in 2018, having evaded justice for more than 35 years. His victims will now never see him in court. They will need to find a path towards healing without a formal finding of guilt.

So much for the Vector, although it could be plotted in considerably greater detail. Examining the character of the abuse itself, its Signature begins to explain how some of the brightest and most powerful young men in the UK could be subjected to violence on a regular basis. Why did their parents, like the trustees who ran the camps, many of them unimpeachably moral characters, choose to protect Smyth rather than the boys?

To answer this question we have to consider the common factors binding everybody into what was going on.

One was a model of parenting that compromised people's ability to offer and receive parental love freely and naturally. Many twentieth-century boarding school boys have struggled with issues arising from parental separation. Mark Stibbe, a Smyth survivor, has movingly described this experience in his book *Home at Last: Freedom from Boarding School Pain*. Boys naturally yearned for a father figure, and some found him in John Smyth.

Another Signature factor was the high tolerance of elitism among everybody involved. Smyth chose the best and brightest, and groomed them into submitting themselves to his brutal and humiliating assaults. To do this he played on their willingness to undergo suffering in order to be the best. This was done in the context of a larger appeal to their need to belong, which they hoped to find in the inner ring within the larger circle of Iwerne campers.

The next element in the mix was the tolerance at the time of punitive behaviour in boarding schools. 'Spare the rod and spoil the child' makes sense in a world informed by punitive theologies that lend themselves to violent abusive practices. Charles Moore, a Conservative journalist, describes the roots of the abuse perpetrated by Smyth. He quotes Andy Morse, a survivor driven to attempting suicide.

> As a child, Smyth was badly beaten by his own father and at his own prep school. Brought up among the Plymouth Brethren, he suffered, Andy believes, from an 'abusive theology'. This imposed a complete rigidity about how life should be lived, and consequently savage punishment for any transgression. In such a mindset, the man wielding the rod may feel more virtuous the harder he hits. In some cases – Smyth's is surely one of them – he derives sexual pleasure from it, so his lusts and his faith become horribly confused.

A few years after being banned from youth work in the UK, Smyth was undertaking it in Zambia. All kinds of amber lights (in Lifton terms) could and should have come on for many adults who knew about Smyth's abuse of Winchester boys and the circumstances of his leaving the country. Yet on 15 December 1992 Guide Nyachuru was found dead in a swimming pool at one of Smyth's camps in Zimbabwe.

The Swiss cheese (James Reason) model of system failure can be applied to this. In order to prevent the death of a vulnerable young person, someone who understood where danger might lie needed to speak out. Someone who knew Smyth's track record should have been willing to ask hard questions about the dangers inherent in what was going on.

Why didn't they? Charles Moore describes another

aspect of the Signature of Smyth's abuse – its basic theological rationale:

> As with the non-violent extremism which gives rise to terrorist attacks, we need to trace the connection between bad ideas and bad actions.

Iwerne boys were heavily drilled in what is called 'Penal Substitutionary Atonement' – the medieval doctrine that Jesus' violent death was punishment for human sin meted out by a righteous God in order to satisfy his wrath. The cross was about propitiating an angry deity, not expiating sins.

This theology was especially appealing in a physically punitive environment like mid-20th century boarding schools, where corporal punishment was still endemic. Iwerne leaders rubbished any critical questioning of this theology as 'woolly liberalism.'

Smyth's abuse represents a massive system failure, theologically and culturally. Somehow nobody claimed the power to challenge Smyth effectively.

At any point along an abuse vector, appropriate interventions can be made. In Mark's case (1), this could have been Stanley the head server questioning the vicar's request to see boys alone for extra training. A parent could have confronted Father Ian. Any one of many senior clerics could have stopped, noticed and intervened. Any of them could have tried to operate the system that theoretically protected Mark. To do this, they did not have to be safeguarding experts, just caring, inquisitive, and objective enough to question possible anomalies.

If theology has been used to validate abuse is the answer simply to ditch theology?

This is to misunderstand the problem. An abuser can use any theology to suspend suspicion and yield access. Signature elements need to be challenged in their own terms. There is no point telling a young man who is being abused using Protestant penal substitution theology that the Pope doesn't like it. If the damage is happening within a context that scores high on Lifton's Mind Control scales, the organisation will simply close ranks and expel the person who has been abused, as a 'heretic.' This will seal the abusee even more tightly into their trap.

Religious leaders can only avoid their theologies being used to damage others if they understand how their own doctrine can be twisted towards abuse. People who lead activities with a tendency towards totalising theology must not drink too heady a draught of their own Kool-Aid. They need to stand back for a moment, examine their beliefs from a potential abuser's point of view, and protect those for whom they have responsibility.

We have seen how totalising groups tend to interpret any external or internal critical attention as hostility. The truth is the exact opposite. Robust critical sense about possible dangers is the only basis on which any activity can flourish. People who run swimming pools should care especially about water safety. Critical awareness of how possible it is to drown in the pool is not an attack on the sport. Wise cycling clubs pay heed to warnings about road safety. They do not resist them as enemy attacks. Critical distance does not wreck either sport. It makes it possible to swim or cycle safely.

Brendan Mooney, in a Facebook comment about the way theology has been weaponised against LGBTI people, has suggested,

> Religious people have often gotten many things right and many things wrong. This does not reduce theology simply to the things that have been wrong. Right now institutional Christianity is facing its shadow side and the harm it has caused.

The best way to disinfect toxic theology is not to ditch all theology, but to develop healthy theology.

One thing is certain. A Church whose leaders refuse to examine their system's potential dangers cannot possibly be safe. What the diocese learned and practised in Mark's case (1) from hunkering down and doing nothing, was summed up devastatingly clearly by Desmond the Dean:

> We've had a few of these down the years and they always blow over. The kid or his parents kick up, but it never goes anywhere. The best way to deal with these people is ignore them. They always go away in the end.

Inertia, complacency and self-deception made the Church fail the Good Samaritan test for Mark. It could easily have done so much better.

5

The Way to the Inn

In recent years all groups working with children and vulnerable adults, including churches, have massively upped their investment in safeguarding. Public institutions, sports clubs and schools, hospitals, churches and media organisations have experienced scandals that show up the inadequacy of what they had assumed to be safe in times gone by. The exposure of Jimmy Savile, Rolf Harris and Stuart Hall has brought this process strikingly into the public domain. Public enquiries have empowered large numbers of people to come forward with experiences that had been sealed up deep within them, wrapped in guilt and shame.

Much abuse has occurred in church in the context of activities involving children, young people and vulnerable adults. The Church of England, like other Churches, has tried to respond to this with major new investment in safeguarding staff and policy. Hundreds of pages of guidelines have been produced. This luxuriant growth of staffing levels and verbiage has not always been experienced as coherent, but there's much more of it than there was twenty years ago.

Various particularities stand out about abuse in church.

First, churches have a large historic mission in relation to children and young people. Even though religious groups have seen a significant collapse in the number of children and young people involved with them, they retain a privileged position in relation to schools in the UK. Many people, disclosing now, experienced their abuse during the last century when churches played a major role in the lives of many children through Sunday schools, choirs, clubs, uniformed organisations and camps. Any danger of abuse is a major turn-off to children and their parents now. Churches who intend to continue working with young people will have to pay attention to what has gone wrong in the past and learn from it. Grovelling apologies for other people's sins and waffle about how it couldn't happen now cannot win people's confidence.

Secondly, churches and religious groups often have cultures of high trust and low accountability, institutionalised through hierarchical attitudes that put leaders on a pedestal and make their behaviour hard to challenge. Surprisingly, many people are still willing to talk with clergy about deeply personal matters. The more people know about others in a networked world, with the sometimes distorting lenses and mirrors of social media, the greater the danger of cynicism. Pulling rank is futile in a less deferential society. It is much easier to lose respect than to win it back. Trust must be cherished and protected, not betrayed. The challenge before the Churches now is one of substance, not presentation. If they want to be trusted they need to work hard to become trustworthy.

Thirdly, churches have been social paradigms in the past, for wider society as well as themselves. Their mission has been about healing, social integration and personal wellbeing. The higher an organisation's pretensions to doing good, the greater the disillusionment when people are betrayed. Churches have claimed to be guardians of popular morality. People outside the Church are disgusted when priests fail to act as such. They could argue that it takes a particular level of hypocrisy to produce errant clergy.

Finally, and in some ways most significantly, the Bible says love must be a matter of deeds, not empty words. The gnostic religions of the ancient world dealt exclusively in rituals, dogma and philosophy. Christianity is about the word made flesh, that is a person not an idea. The letter of James points out how futile it is to wish victims well whilst doing nothing materially to help them:

> What good is it, my brothers and sisters, if you say you have faith but do not have works? Can faith save you? If a brother or sister is naked and lacks daily food, and one of you says to them, 'Go in peace; keep warm and eat your fill,' and yet you do not supply their bodily needs, what is the good of that? So faith by itself, if it has no works, is dead. (James 2:14-17)

A Church that deals in aspirations and ideals alone is betraying its own faith. Two hundred and fifty years ago, Ann Radcliffe laid down an important principle:

> I never trust people's assertions, I always judge of them by their actions. (*The Mysteries of Udolpho*, 1764)

Good leadership can be recognised by high levels of trust, integrity and relationships. In recent years there has been much aspirational hufflepuff in the Church of England about 'Leadership' as the answer to its problems. People gauge a leader's trustworthiness on the basis of their actions and practice, not their public relations or grovelling skills. How we behave to one another is far more significant than operational success (in a narrow sense), or numbers.

Increasingly since 2010, Church of England bishops have expressed a fine intention to put survivors first. 'Safe Spaces' is a project that attempts to take their experiences seriously in a pastorally sensitive way. Unfortunately, nothing much has come of it in years of tinkering. Five years on, the Church cannot relax control over the process sufficiently to win survivors' confidence. The project still seems to have no adequate budget from a Church that spends hundreds of millions of pounds on its own pet missional projects. Many survivors feel the Church dishes up virtuous rhetoric that sounds increasingly empty as its skeletons rattle in the closet. Fulsome apologies without changed behaviour soon begin to annoy survivors.

One survivor, listening to an abject apology from the archbishop, has said to us 'I don't care how upset and ashamed he is. This is not about him or his feelings. What I need is for him to meet me, take responsibility and actually do something.'

In February 2018, General Synod members were given a booklet compiled by Andrew Graystone, a journalist who has worked closely with many abuse survivors. Its title was a striking allusion to Jesus' Sermon on the Mount – *We asked for bread but you gave us stones – Victims of abuse address the church in their own words*. In it, public statements from senior bishops are printed in brown. The Archbishop of Canterbury's words acknowledged there is a long way to go and promised a better future:

> The victims are the people we care about most. They really, really matter…
>
> The culture around how survivors of abuse are heard has in effect been to tell them to be quiet, and to keep away from the love of Christ …
>
> … to address the whole culture of silencing in the Church is vital because failure to do so is a form of abuse for the second time, as bad if not worse than the first betrayal.

The Archbishop himself, helpfully, attended a survivors' vigil on the Saturday morning of the synod and stood alongside them.

In *We asked for bread but you gave us stones*, however, senior bishops' fine words are surrounded by a sea of blue print in which survivors describe their experiences of dealing with the Church. One or two pay tribute to kind individuals including archdeacons and safeguarding advisors, but overwhelmingly the blue paragraphs contain disturbing accounts of pastoral failures:

> My abuser was listened to and loved. I was treated as guilty. They hoped I'd go away. They covered their inadequate tracks. It's hard listening to them preach – it makes me want to stand up and shout that they are lying. One of them even turned and walked the other way to avoid me.
>
> The C of E has been incredibly unhelpful. It is now six years since I first reported abuse, and I have no idea who is 'dealing with me.' I have been passed around, like I am the troublemaker. They have been devoid of compassion.
>
> It has been the failure of anyone, including bishops, to say 'Are you OK?

At the next General Synod meeting, in July 2018, survivors were allowed to organise an evening fringe meeting attended by both Archbishops, and to speak for themselves. Next day one survivor, Jo Kind, was invited to make a presentation during a synod debate, something previously pronounced impossible, forbidden by its standing orders. Both these events, and the Archbishop of Canterbury's genuine interest and attendance at what must have been a difficult meeting, seemed great signs of progress.

Every silver lining has a cloud, however. Next day one diocesan bishop decided to threaten a survivor of rape in one of his diocese's vicarages with legal action for suggesting his counselling support had been capped as, in fact, it had been. This silly bit of sabre rattling was formally pointless, but it somewhat took the edge off rejoicing after what had otherwise been a positive weekend. The Church was obviously not quite out of the woods yet.

It seems the Church is finding it very difficult to give

real substance to its fine words. Various themes recur in survivors' bad experiences.

Many speak of more or less unwitting denial, blanking and cover-up. Perhaps people heavily invested in the institution find it hard to understand how their beloved Church could harm people. Perhaps much obfuscation and delay is caused when files are parked in the 'too-difficult box'. Perhaps Desmond the Cathedral Dean is simply reporting his experience when he says that the best way to deal with these people is to ignore them because they always go away in the end. It is exhausting, physically mentally and spiritually, for survivors to have to drive everything themselves, always and everywhere. Meanwhile it often seems that senior clerics are just covering their ears, mouthing occasional apologies, and sitting on their hands.

Survivors do sometimes experience kind and constructive pastoral care. When this happens, it can be immensely healing. It is bad experiences that need to change, however, not good ones. The whole picture is very inconsistent. It depends partly on which one of 42 dioceses are involved, how many of them, and the people involved. It is a very bitty picture.

It is almost inevitable that people in such a complex multi-layered structure will find it easy to evade responsibility and blame others, including victims. People who engage positively with victims of abuse in church are sometimes told they should hold back from survivors 'because they are very damaged people'. Of course they are. It was often the Church that damaged them! The question is whether their hurt is something for which the people at the top feel any responsibility. It also seems that local churches find it easier to offer kindness and understanding than senior officials and clergy.

Some survivors feel they are scapegoats for the institution's pastoral failures. Lurking in the shadows behind this is often a strong strand of religious exceptionalism. If members of the public bought food that made them ill, they would expect speedy appropriate redress. But the Church seems to consider itself to be different, with no need to provide the responsiveness, accountability, and ethical practice people expect on the high street.

Often it feels as though the Church's primary concern is its image. And when it does act, it feels like a Rolls Royce with a lawn mower engine and powerful brakes, a microscopic dirty windscreen and a huge rear view mirror.

To help feed constructive imagination around this problem we have translated some of the things Church officials have allegedly said to survivors into the more familiar world of supermarket ready-meals. A shop that told customers with food poisoning that it was their own fault, and to go away, would not expect to carry on in business. We propose that those responding to disclosures think before they react, having applied the 'Bad Lasagne' test we present in a fuller form in Appendix 4 (pp. 198-201 below).

We asked for bread but you gave us stones asked a simple question – 'What could the church do better to help victims of abuse like yourself?' B, a male survivor suggested:

> respond quickly and take questions seriously. Put survivors first. Create a fair and just reparation structure. Recognise impact on our lives. Listen and learn from the expertise of survivors. Involve survivors in creating a culture focused on healing – not protection of institution. Become honest. Stop the denial culture.

Q, another male survivor was more succinct:

> Listen to survivors. Work with us, rather than as enemies, to learn lessons so that things can be better for future victims.

For A, a female survivor, the heart of the matter was simple:

> Pretty much respond like the gospel message not the legal Pharisees.

But how?

Survivors speak of a 'broken church,' and we do not wish to evade the force of their experience by minimising the problems around safeguarding in any way. We have felt at times a kind of despair about the scope and scale of our Church's failure as a pastoral organisation, that we know others share.

The worst response of all, however, would be paralysis, fed by a feeling this is all just too big to do anything about. There is no simple way forward, but it would be tragic if people just gave up trying. There are areas of systemic policy and practice on which progress must be made.

Small marginal gains

In 2002, British Cycling tasked Sir Dave Brailsford with improving the sport's languishing fortunes. The GB team had only won a single Olympic gold medal in its 76 year history. Six years later at the 2008 Beijing Olympics his squad won 7 out of the available 10 gold medals, a feat the team matched at the 2012 London Olympics.

But how?

Brailsford approached the problem in a radical way:

> It struck me that we should think small, not big, and adopt a philosophy of continuous improvement through the aggregation of marginal gains. Forget about perfection. Focus on progression and compound the improvements. (Interview by Even Harrell, *Harvard Business Review,* October 30 2015)

A policy of small marginal gains would not, of course, enable a non-cyclist to win the Tour de France next year. This model can only be applied with the greatest of caution to a Church which, unlike the British Cycling Team, could not be said to be at the top of its game.

That said, there are resonances. Safeguarding, like cycling, is an endeavour in which perfection, however desirable, is impossible. Religious leaders, like top cyclists, are often so deeply immersed in their work that they become neurotic and obsessional. They chase a perfection that seems perpetually to elude them partly because everything is inter-related.

Brailsford sought a mere 1% improvement in every part of the sport. Could small marginal gains, aggregated across the board, help safeguarding too? Some may be easy, whilst others are hard to imagine, let alone achieve. They are all interrelated so progress in any would move things forward.

Survivors' bad experiences of Church indicate seven practical areas where significant gains could be achieved.

1. Spiritual abuse

Religion can play a very powerful role in many lives. When people turn to the church in times of crisis this heightens the level of vulnerability. Many churches are very good at helping needy people. When things go wrong, however, they go catastrophically wrong.

A new language is developing around this phenomenon which names it as 'spiritual abuse' This area has been clarified and opened up considerably by the groundbreaking work of Lisa Oakley, Kathryn Kinmond, and others.

> Spiritual abuse is a form of emotional and psychological abuse. It is characterised by a systematic pattern of coercive and controlling behaviour in a religious context. Spiritual

abuse can have a deeply damaging impact on those who experience it.

> This abuse may include: manipulation and exploitation, enforced accountability, censorship of decision-making, the requirement of secrecy and silence, coercion to conform, control through the use of sacred texts or teaching, the requirement of obedience to the abuser, the suggestion that the abuser has a 'divine' position, isolation as a means of punishment, and superiority and elitism. (CT 22.08.2018)

Until very recently the very existence of spiritual abuse was contested. The first legal case alleging it was brought under the Clergy Discipline Measure 2003 against The Revd Timothy Davis, an Oxfordshire vicar. In January 2018 he was found to have committed spiritual abuse against a teenage boy whom he had dominated by a highly controlling discipleship and mentoring scheme.

The Evangelical Alliance was not happy about the concept. In an interview for Premier Christian Radio the chair of its Theology Advisory Group Revd Dr David Hilborn said to the journalist Toia Mbakwe:

> What we want to do is say that there is psychological abuse, there's emotional abuse.
> That's well defined legally. There's case law on that. Let's accept that sometimes that might take place on church premises and sometimes that might not.

The interview was given in the context of a major survey of churchgoers by the Churches' Child Protection Advisory Service (now thirtyyone:eight). Two thirds of respondents claimed to have experienced spiritual abuse.

Jayne Ozanne and Vicky Beeching have both described as spiritual abuse their Christian communities' efforts to 'cure' them of their homosexuality. These involved intense prayer and laying on of hands, courses, and specific types of pseudo psychotherapy. It goes without saying that none of these produced a 'cure'. All of them caused pain and suffering.

The extraordinary power of spiritual abuse lies in its ability to outsource responsibility for the misuse of power. Everything is done in the name of God and obedience to Scripture. The pain, if the victims did but know it, is an expression of God's love that will somehow do them good in the end. Those who are in reality being abusive often have an utter belief that they are but the agents of God and to question them is to question God himself. Jesus himself warned his followers against this kind of behaviour:

> An hour is coming when those who kill you will think that by doing so they are offering worship to God. (John 16:3)

An objective observer would be able to see that Ryan and Bethany (10) were being groomed. Spiritual abuse was taking place. The sincerity of the couple's Christian commitment made them both vulnerable to the skilled weaponising of Scripture against them. They accepted a degree of control over their lives which was not healthy. As people who came to church longing to hear directly from God they were drawn to a heroic leader speaking with supreme confidence. It was utterly beguiling, especially to Ryan. Critical faculties were switched off. Abusive control, as in any cult, destroyed their relationship in the end.

Karen's domestic abuse (5) had spiritual roots. She had spiritual reasons to tolerate and excuse David's behaviour. These were very real to her and blinded her to what was really going on. Her friend Angela made a totally unreasonable and misguided promise to keep quiet. Again it was motivated by loyalty to a spiritual agenda. It is always very hard to break out from domestic abuse, but extra spiritual bonding produces enduring violence and cruelty at another level. The power of being told what God is supposed to think is immense: 'You made this unbreakable promise before God and it is your duty to forgive your husband and support him in his work for the Lord.'

The woman quoted earlier who did not find it easy talking to a bishop about the Church's lack of care for her whilst in a violent and abusive marriage recognised that 'of course it was the theology that did it'.

She was right. It is not possible to separate spiritual abuse from its theological roots. This type of abuse is so powerful because of the victim's commitment to their faith combined with the abuser's outsourcing to God of their moral responsibility. This is how gay 'conversion therapy' works. The person exerting inappropriate power believes what they are doing is God's will. This could be life-controlling discipling as experienced by Ryan and Bethany (10). Here obedience to a controlling individual was expressed as obedience to God.

This often happens in religion. People in positions of power genuinely believe they have a God-given understanding of the divine purpose for someone else's life. When you are told that this is what God wants it is very difficult to resist. When rooted in an essentially violent theology this sort of spiritual abuse becomes very dangerous and even life-threatening. As with all abuse, death by suicide can never be ruled out.

A new and deeper understanding of spiritual abuse is crucial for the Church to get the rest of its response system right. The people who have been abused have not simply experienced a physical or emotional attack. They have had the core of their identity, their whole understanding of what life is about, their firmest commitment to God, manipulated and exploited. It is no surprise that both Vicky Beeching and Jayne Ozanne went on to suffer severe breakdowns of health, both physical and mental.

Norman (14) had a terrible experience when he came out in his twenties, so bad that he and Daniel, his partner, vowed never to go to church again. After Daniel died, Norman, in his loneliness and emptiness, felt drawn back to church. He believed the apologies and assurances that things had changed. He was shocked when Phil, the prayer minister, still wanted to pray for his 'healing'. Worse still, despite assurances to the contrary, Brian the new vicar was still comfortable with homophobic preaching from his pulpit by a visiting Link Missionary.

This is not to question Phil or Brian's sincerity. Norman did not come to church to experience politeness, but to be affirmed as the child of God he dared to believe he might be. The healing was in that affirmation. St Oscar Romero asks:

> By what right have we catalogued persons as first class persons or second class persons? In the theology of human nature there is only one class: children of God.

It followed that Norman could not experience the kind of genteel Schrodinger's existence on offer at St Peter's, affirmed by half the congregation but rubbished by the other half, as anything other than reabuse.

For the Church to address issues of spiritual abuse the first task is education. Most churchgoers' instincts are perfectly good. They might feel uncomfortable in the presence of spiritual abuse, but there is no scale against which to measure their feelings. They end up thinking their discomfort is just them, or an aspect of how things are meant to be. If spiritual abuse were openly discussed and its boundaries became clear, then everyone would feel more confident about challenging it.

This would make it possible to resist being manipulated by the inappropriate twisting and aiming of Scripture at particular people. Spiritual abuse using Scripture occurs at various levels from the intensely personal to the national. There are many instances of this in our tales from the crypt, and we have listed some of the most pernicious and pervasive of these we have encountered and not described elsewhere in Appendix 5 (Pages 201-204 below).

Crazy things happen on a personal level when the Bible is misused. Few of Jesus' male followers have managed to sustain his generally open and equal attitude towards women. Religion in general has a very bad track record for sustaining violence towards women:

> Religion, in many women's lives, has been a force, if not the primary force, in shaping our acceptance of abuse. And as such it has sustained violence against women. (Susan Tang, quoted by Elaine Storkey, *Scars across humanity: understanding and overcoming violence against women*, 2015, p. 187)

In June 2013 *Huffington Post* exposed a US Evangelical website called 'Christian Domestic Discipline.' It commended practices including 'Maintenance Discipline':

> Discipline, usually spanking, given at regular intervals for the purpose of maintaining a submissive mindset in a wife, correcting minor faults and/or reinforcing marital roles...
>
> Some wives have an extreme need to 'feel' their husband's authority on a regular basis, and for some of them, play spanking is not enough. It needs to be something 'real'...
>
> Some wives have a difficult time maintaining a submissive mindset towards their husband. Regular maintenance spankings can go a long way towards keeping

her heart softened and willing to surrender to her husband's leadership.

Some leadership! This extreme form of so-called 'Complementarianism' is an abuser's charter:

> Whether to use maintenance or not is a decision best left up to the individual couple. Though it is ultimately the decision of the husband, he should be careful to take into consideration his wife's thoughts, actions, and reactions to maintenance discipline.

The CDD page quotes Hebrews 12:11 to support this nonsense:

> Now no chastening for the present seemeth to be joyous, but grievous: nevertheless afterwards it yeildeth the peaceable fruit of righteousness unto them which are exercised thereby.

Public reaction to this 'biblical' lifestyle choice was strong enough for those who advocated it to take the site down sometime after 2014.

There have been, and still are, Christians who quote Scripture to support beating their children, a practice which most people now recognise as child abuse. In November 2001, a High Court judge rejected a plea by a Christian school in Merseyside to review the ban on corporal punishment in Section 548 of the Education Act 1996. Phil Williamson, the school's head was not convinced:

> What we are saying is for some issues in disciplining children, there is a Biblical mandate there for it.

Scripture has also been misused at higher levels. Hanging was effectively abolished in the UK in 1965. The House of Commons had voted for abolition almost twenty years earlier but bishops in the House of Lords quoted Scripture to block legislation for a generation.

The remedy for misuse of Scripture is good interpretation of the text. This requires education at all levels, but an important starting point is theological colleges and courses. Clarity about the danger of spiritual abuse would establish a far higher ethic. Manipulative preaching and teaching, along with heavy controlling discipling, would be recognised more easily for what they are.

All too often people whose deepest commitments have been manipulated simply leave the Church. Spiritual abuse has to be named when it happens, and offenders dealt with to avert danger to others. When this does not happen, many lose all religious faith. Fuelled by anger at the unjust treatment they have experienced, they can end up in a strange kind of limbo. There was something of this in Norman's experience (14). He consciously rejected the Church, but the power of his religious formation drew him back in a time of crisis. This conflicted feeling, like running anti-church software on a church operating system, is doubly confusing and painful.

Each diocese has its own spiritual dynamic. Each bishop has their own working style, and some of these normalise abusive behaviour as 'strong' or 'biblical' leadership. It is quite possible, however hard this may be to acknowledge, for a bishop to be spiritually abusive in an unaccountable way. Some use Scripture to control their clergy on the basis of an internalised feeling that, because they are a bishop, what they think must be right.

Spiritual abuse is bigger than any single diocese. There is an overwhelming need for external accountability. Someone who is not invested in any particular bishop's world can stand outside it. They have a far better chance of recognising what is going on and are less likely to spiritualise the problem away.

Ryan and Bethany's relationship (10) might have survived if other people within the community had been able to spot what was going on and report it. In a non-Christian environment Rufus's behaviour towards them could more easily have been recognised as grooming. Under a dense blanket of God-talk, it remained hidden.

Most people who have experienced spiritual abuse run a mile from any church. Many more stories need to be told. There are healthy new conversations beginning about spiritual abuse, but as yet no practical toolkit for recognising it has fully developed.

2. Mandatory Reporting

The idea is very simple. Anyone who believes abuse may have occurred, or receives a disclosure of it, must, by law, report it to someone in an organisation with appropriate professional skills and training. The safeguarding lead can then assess the matter and act accordingly.

The Diocesan Safeguarding and Clergy Discipline Measure 2016 nods towards the principle:

> A relevant person must have due regard to guidance issued by the House of Bishops on matters relating to the safeguarding of children and vulnerable adults. (Section 5.1)

In practice, however, the wording is such that the legal duty this imposes is almost always underestimated. One person's 'due regard' could seem to another like passing by on the other side. The concept is certainly fluid, and those who fail to report appear to face no sanction.

A clear and unequivocal obligation of Mandatory Reporting relieves people of any uncertainty about what they should do. A churchwarden like Angela was sworn to secrecy about Karen's domestic abuse (5). If she had been obliged to say something, Karen might have received the help she needed.

In a video released in September 2018, Andy Morse, a survivor of John Smyth's Iwerne camps abuse whilst at Winchester, relates movingly the dilemma he and his parents faced about revealing what had happened to the police. His loving parents said they would be guided by him in their response. At the time he could not manage the thought of police involvement. Therefore the crime went unreported for many years. Looking back at his experience neither he nor his parents would necessarily make the same decision today. Lack of mandatory reporting forced his family to have to make a choice they should never have had to. Had there been a legal obligation to report his abuse, matters would have been dealt with differently. John Smyth could well have stood trial, and the law would have relieved the family from an onerous decision.

In the present state of the law, reporting concerns is often an opaque and haphazard business. Mark (1) reported his abuse to his mother and was told off for it. Further disclosures to senior clergy were not pursued. Insofar as diocesan figures took them seriously, they tried to investigate in-house and passed nothing on to the authorities.

The effect of a mandatory reporting law would be to change the default position from not reporting to making the story known to someone who should be able to do something about it. They then decide what, if anything, needs to be done.

The point is that information flow is not stymied from the off. The anomaly, having been identified, can be acted upon.

The transformational effect of this approach can be measured by the impact of Childline, run by the NSPCC.

This was set up by journalist and TV presenter Esther Rantzen in 1986 after viewers responded to a survey on child abuse, and the related helpline was inundated with calls. Childline gives children a safe place to report experiences and concerns to someone other than the abuser or an abuser's professional associate. On its first night it received over 50,000 calls. In 2017/18, Childline provided over 278,000 counselling sessions to children and young people with over 3.1 million hits on its website.

Churches often run on discretion and deference, weak boundaries and a commendable will to think the best of everyone. Clever abusers groom communities as well as victims and those around them. Mandatory Reporting cuts through all that with the force of law.

One of the greatest reductions in UK road deaths since the 1960s has been the consequence of enforcing drink driving law. Everyone knew for years that drink driving was dangerous. Since 1925 it had been a criminal offence to be found drunk in charge of any mechanically propelled vehicle on any highway or in a public place. The Highway Code provided a code of practice to which due regard was required. Unfortunately, people had their own ways of complying, or not. It was only after 1967 when compliance was clearly defined and mandatory that the position actually improved.

Mandatory Reporting is not a magic bullet, however. It raises questions, too.

Who do people report to?

This will usually be a safeguarding lead, but it could be a helpline or senior professional, police officer or social worker. What matters is that disclosures are made to people who will respond appropriately. For Mandatory Reporting to work people have to have confidence in those to whom they disclose.

Who does it apply to?

Legally speaking, the answer has to be anyone involved in a controlled activity – one that gives privileged personal contact to children or vulnerable adults. In church this has to include office holders like churchwardens and organists as well as clergy.

When is a disclosure a disclosure?

The answer can sometimes be obvious. A person witnesses someone sexually assaulting somebody else. If they know it is illegal not to report what they have seen the question of what to do answers itself.

But what about a disclosure relating to the past? Until very recently many believed that any case where the alleged abuser was no longer active or alive was 'historic'. No case, however, can be historic as long as it affects anyone's life.

If in the course of a dinner party a conversation turns to a recent documentary and one of the guests says, 'My choirmaster at prep school did that', how should this be treated? It would seem sensible to check privately with the guest whether they saw this as a new disclosure and what response they wanted.

Revealing personal information is always stressful. Every disclosure involves reliving trauma. Someone may well test the waters in an oblique way before saying much directly. Nobody is perfect, and a glancing disclosure may sometimes be missed, especially in a conversation about something else. In principle it should not be. Mandatory Reporting would make this clear and create a safer environment for all.

What happens when someone reports?

Survivors often feel a loss of autonomy when they disclose. This is a crucial moment, and people need encouragement to reach it, and intensive support once they do. Reporting should not put them on a travelator that compromises their confidentiality and reduces them to being a case over which they have no control. Neither should it force them into a process in which they have to re-encounter their abuser.

Core Groups are a concept borrowed from Social Work to co-ordinate the Church's response to reports of abuse. They usually include archdeacons, safeguarding advisers, lawyers and reputation managers. Insurers have sometimes been included, too. Survivors are usually not represented on them. Their focus appears to be managing the situation in order to minimise damage to the Church's reputation. Once a core group starts up, many survivors find themselves excluded from their own story.

More seriously, survivors lose control over their deeply sensitive personal information. They do not even know who is in their core group, and leaks easily occur. The Church is a small and highly networked world in which gossip is rife, as Lucy (15) discovered. She had no idea of the number of people to whom her information had been communicated.

A critical question arises: who are Core Groups *for?* If they are fundamentally case management tools for the benefit of the Church, not those whose lives are under the microscope, it is hardly surprising that they induce suspicion and anger in survivors. Reducing a human being to a case inevitably dehumanises them. This is something the Archbishop of Canterbury has rightly said the Church does not wish to do.

Unfortunately, as the 2017 Carlile Review of the handling of the George Bell allegations reveals, core groups have often been constituted with intermittent membership and insufficient meetings to keep track of the material.

Core groups that only meet haphazardly, with a variable membership, cannot achieve much. They need qualified members who meet often enough to do a proper job. This means a pool of many well trained chairs and members to make them up. There also needs to be clarity and honesty about their purpose. This is not to spin the news and save face, or to manage the complainant as a problem, but to determine what has happened and co-ordinate a timely response.

There is, perhaps, another way. Permanent multidisciplinary professional teams which included survivors' representatives alongside social workers, pastors, communicators, lawyers and forensic specialists, answerable to diocesan safeguarding committees, could probably provide a far more stable and effective response than the present *ad hoc* arrangements.

Core Groups as presently constituted would no longer be needed. Unless serious attention is paid to concerns about them it is impossible to see how the Archbishop's good intentions can be fulfilled.

Mandatory Reporting – Why not?

On 26 June 2014 Paul Butler, then the Church's safeguarding lead bishop, endorsed Mandatory Reporting during a debate in the House of Lords.

> Far too many cases of abuse could have been prevented if professional people who had serious suspicions of abuse were required to report it to a relevant authority. There remains too much fear of whistleblowing or of being thought of as interfering. Mandatory reporting for professional staff would alleviate any doubts and prevent people from asking themselves, 'Should I or shouldn't I?'. Suspicions should not be brushed aside or left unheeded. The time for mandatory reporting has arrived.

Since then, however, the trail has gone cold. The Church seems confused about how to take matters forward.

There has long been a diversity of views among social work professionals about mandatory reporting. Some resist it from fear that the volume of complaints would overwhelm them, and generate a large number of additional spurious accusations.

These fears seem short sighted and self-serving. If Mandatory Reporting were to reveal more cases that would surely be the whole point. The government would not disband the anti-terrorist squad on the grounds that it was detecting too many terrorists.

An early surge in numbers could happen, as it did when Childline was launched, but numbers would find their own level soon enough. If Mandatory Reporting produced false positives, those who handled disclosures would have to become clearer and more competent in dealing with them. That could hardly be a bad thing, either.

It is notoriously difficult to talk about abuse, so anything that lowers the reporting threshold has to be good news. Cases the Church doesn't yet know about cannot be hidden indefinitely. The level of resourcing required to sort out the aftermath of Peter Ball's abuse is very much greater than would have been necessary had the Church authorities collaborated fully with the police in the first place.

In fact there is no evidence that Mandatory Reporting would produce an overwhelming torrent of false positives. A major study has found that only a tiny number of false positives occur in an Australian system based on Mandatory Reporting.

Sex offences are crimes. One legacy from the Troubles is that Mandatory Reporting already applies to crime in Northern Ireland. Yet there has been no tsunami of crime reports there. Since 2015 Mandatory reporting has applied to suspected Female Genital Mutilation in England and Wales. This is a measure of how seriously the law now takes FGM, if not sexual abuse.

If we really want to make churches safe for children and vulnerable people, it is hard to argue against what Paul

Butler, the Bishop of Durham, said in the House of Lords in 2014. A Mandatory Reporting law would require clarity about whom to report to. Those receiving disclosures would need, as now, adequate training and support to do their job.

In conspiracy thrillers someone reports corruption or malpractice to their superiors only to find that the person to whom they've reported it is, in fact, part of the conspiracy. The only way to prevent this is to make sure that the person to whom anomalies are reported is truly independent. Consideration of this leads to another area that requires attention and improvement, Independence.

3. Independence

There is a growing demand for transparency in public life, and clear lines of accountability. But to whom? All public entities, government, police, schools, health services, even private companies, are under intense pressure to throw open their doors and windows to outside scrutiny.

In 1989, 97 Liverpool Football Fans were killed in a crush at Hillsborough Stadium. For many years survivors and their families battled against cultures of coverup and self-protection among police, local government and the media. Major police inquiries were held, but justice remained elusive. Bishop James Jones led an independent review of the incident and the way it had been handled that reported in November 2017. *The patronising disposition of unaccountable power* catalogues a woeful tale of denial, excuses and corruption on the part of various public and private authorities.

The Hillsborough Inquiry proposed a six point charter for victims.

1. In the event of a public tragedy, activate its emergency plan and deploy its resources to rescue victims, to support the bereaved and to protect the vulnerable.
2. Place the public interest above our own reputation.

3. Approach forms of public scrutiny – including public inquiries and inquests – with candour, in an open, honest and transparent way, making full disclosure of relevant documents, material and facts. Our objective is to assist the search for the truth. We accept that we should learn from the findings of external scrutiny and from past mistakes.

4. Avoid seeking to defend the indefensible or to dismiss or disparage those who may have suffered where we have fallen short.

5. Ensure all members of staff treat members of the public and each other with mutual respect and with courtesy. Where we fall short, we should apologise straightforwardly and genuinely.

6. Recognise that we are accountable and open to challenge. We will ensure that processes are in place to allow the public to hold us to account for the work we do and for the way in which we do it. We do not knowingly mislead the public or the media.

The Church has made considerable progress in developing complex policy and procedural rigmarole, but has found it harder to engage with survivors. Many of them say their experience of the Church of England has fallen well short of the Hillsborough Charter.

The professional guardians of the sacred have seemed consumed by a desire to protect themselves and the reputation of the institution they represent. Again and again survivors have had to struggle to the point of exhaustion, making all the running, wading through a quagmire of guff curated by shadowy but obstructive authority figures.

The Church of England still can't quite bring itself to

Recognise that we are accountable and open to challenge. We will ensure that processes are in place to allow the public to hold us to account for the work we do and for the way in which we do it.

Individual experiences of personal kindness abound, but the corporate response remains 'the patronising disposition of unaccountable power'.

Gordon Baron, a Hillsborough family member, described police internal inquiries in these terms:

> The IPCC and Operation Resolve investigations might have good intentions but it's still 'the police investigating the police' and this makes me suspicious and not confident.

Until Inquiries are independent and seen to be independent people will not be able to trust them. Why should any public institution expect to get away with marking its own homework? Independence in some form seems inescapable if the Church is to win back its credibility as a safe and honourable place.

Practically and politically independence may be necessary, but there are also strong theological and missional arguments for more transparency in the Church.

Jesus spoke of the coming Kingdom as a place of no secrets – 'What you hear whispered, proclaim from the housetops.' (Matthew 10:27)

In St John's Gospel Jesus clarifies the dynamics of obsessional secrets and lies:

> this is the judgment, that the light has come into the world, and people loved darkness rather than light because their deeds were evil. For all who do evil hate the light and do not come to the light, so that their deeds may not be exposed. But those who do what is true come to the light, so that it may be clearly seen that their deeds have been done in God. (John 3:19-21)

Jesus' enemies plot against him secretly. In contrast the Christian community walks in the light.

> Nothing in all creation is hidden from God's sight. Everything is uncovered and laid bare before the eyes of the one to whom we must give account. (Hebrews 3:13)

When the Church walks in the light, it fulfils its primary purpose by living out Kingdom values.

Many church people see external oversight of their safeguarding as a secular imposition. This view has very deep historic roots. In 1170 Thomas Becket died for the rights and privileges of the Church. One of these was the right of clergy to avoid common law justice by claiming 'benefit of clergy.' This meant being tried in the bishops' courts for offences including murder and rape, where the penalty would be limited to a severe penance. Old habits die hard, but the Church of England is a reformed church.

Some people object to independent oversight on non-medieval grounds. They suggest that the Church could not own its responsibility for safeguarding if outsiders were too involved.

How weird is that? The Church does not clamour for benefit of clergy when it comes to fire regulations, drink drive laws, or accountants' reporting standards. In all these areas it is perfectly happy to trust secular authority to do its job.

The state has a duty to protect all citizens. Most abuse is, in fact, crime. Christians surely should have no qualms about involving the police in criminal investigation. St Paul taught, indeed, that Christians have a God-given duty to collaborate with the state in matters of justice:

> Let every person be subject to the governing authorities; for there is no authority except from God, and those authorities

that exist have been instituted by God. Therefore whoever resists authority resists what God has appointed, and those who resist will incur judgment. For rulers are not a terror to good conduct, but to bad. Do you wish to have no fear of the authority? Then do what is good, and you will receive its approval; for it is God's servant for your good. But if you do what is wrong, you should be afraid, for the authority does not bear the sword in vain! It is the servant of God to execute wrath on the wrongdoer. Therefore one must be subject, not only because of wrath but also because of conscience. (Romans 13)

One text is open to misuse here. In 1 Corinthians 6 St Paul upbraids Christians who have taken their disputes to secular courts. He seems to lay down a principle that the Church's dirty linen should never be washed by unbelievers.

It is important to notice two points about this passage.

Firstly, St Paul does not say that Christians should avoid courts because justice doesn't matter. He says the exact opposite. Christians, in his colourful phrase, are to judge the angels. Therefore their standards of justice should be higher than those of any secular court. There is no excuse here, then, for processes that are loaded unjustly against someone who has been wronged in church.

Secondly, 1 Corinthians 6 is about civil claims. If church abuse can ever be regarded as a falling out between believers, there is always inequality involved. Its power dynamics cannot be anything like a dispute between equal neighbours over a garden fence.

And yet, sadly, some Christians continue to cover up crime within the fellowship. John Smyth QC was credibly alleged to have committed acts that, at the time, fell under the Offences Against the Person Act 1861 Section 47. Shockingly, the trustees of the charity he had led covered up, obstructed the police, facilitated Smyth's relocation to

Africa, and then supported him in a new venture identical to the one he had been banned from in the UK. Had his original wrongdoing been (mandatorily) reported none of this could have happened. A shameful 35 year coverup would have been prevented. The Church and charity's reputations would have been enhanced not diminished by independence.

What should independence look like in Church of England safeguarding? Good progress has been made in recent years with audit, risk assessment, and case review.

The Church has invested significantly in safeguarding in the past decade. Its national team has expanded from a single part timer to a small department. How can the public have confidence that this increased resource is being well used? To be consistent and effective safeguarding activity requires a robust process of auditing.

The Church has engaged the Social Care Institute for Excellence to conduct simple procedural audits in every diocese. Some interesting and useful technical observations have been recorded and acted upon. Many dioceses, for example, have learnt they are behind with their training programmes. The SCIE recommendations encourage improvement.

That said, they have been advisory and low-level. One Diocesan Safeguarding Advisor's handwriting was illegible. SCIE recommended that the diocese might care to transcribe its records of disclosure, or at any rate, the names of people in them, but only if the Diocesan Board of Finance felt it could afford it.

More concerningly, none of these reviews engaged in work with survivors. This was held to be beyond their remit. This is not to impugn the professionalism of SCIE. In all fields of human endeavour those who pay the piper call the tune. A SCIE survey of survivor experience was thrown together in a hurry for the July 2018 General Synod. Some survivors hoped it could run for a longer period whilst others were concerned about the way it was set up with no reference to an ethics committee. The survey was probably the best that could be managed, given the resource and time constraints laid down by the Church that commissioned it. Here lies the rub.

Without a genuinely independent auditing process there is nobody external to mandate and monitor basic record keeping discipline, good listening to survivors, or even adequate funding to complete a survey properly.

Another area which requires independent involvement is the regular task of assessing individuals who may pose a risk to children or vulnerable adults. The Church has made more progress here than elsewhere. There is a well-worn path to various agencies who have developed appropriate expertise. There is a centrally held list of good practitioners, and it seems effective use is often being made of them.

All is not quite as it could be, though. Risks can only be assessed in the first place for cases that have been reported. Reporting practice is widely variable across the Church. Furthermore, dioceses can be anxious about the high cost of risk assessments. National and diocesan safeguarding budgets have grown but we cannot be sure that some cases for which a risk assessment should have been undertaken have not been overlooked. Only an independent body could assess the scale of this problem.

Risk assessments are pointless unless they are acted upon. One bishop commissioned a professional assessment for a clergy person that found him to present a significant risk to women. The cleric was told that after successful completion of a course of counselling, he would need a follow-up assessment to confirm his progress with the issues that caused the problem. He could then resume active ministry. This approach did not suit him. The bishop in the diocese next door was briefed on the position but decided to ignore advice and give a green light anyway.

Progress has also been made in reviewing past cases, with varying degrees of independence.

The Elliott Review considered the way in which the Church had dealt with a survivor of criminal abuse by a London priest who was also a well-known ecclesiastical lawyer. He was also abused by someone who was subsequently promoted and became a bishop. It was delivered by Ian Elliott, one of the world's leading safeguarding experts and former head of the NSPCC in Northern Ireland. He has worked in this area with churches all over the world, including with the Roman Catholic Church in Ireland, and is not, himself, an Anglican. He was truly independent as well as massively competent to conduct a review of this case.

So far so good. The Church appeared to accept his recommendations and even appointed a (then) junior bishop to monitor and report on progress after a year. The Elliott review's training recommendations had indeed been attended to substantially, but these were low hanging fruit.

The recommendations about survivor response were acknowledged and occasionally acted upon. The parts of the report that involved major cultural change, reporting and independence, were quietly shelved.

By the report's two year anniversary the Elliott review was being rubbished on the quiet by senior church civil servants. Despite the fact that the Archbishop of Canterbury had given his personal mandate to the implementation of this review's recommendations, one senior bishop even told the survivor at the heart of it:

> Of course we're under any obligation to carry out every recommendation of any independent review.

Also, by then other case reviews had been produced, many by faithful Anglicans with less independence. Those were fixed on officially, with some relief, instead. No second anniversary progress report was produced for the Elliott Review.

The virtue of independent case reviewing is accepted by everybody involved. It is time consuming but vital work if the Church is to learn from its mistakes.

That said, there needs to be a genuine commitment to implement change as a result of what is revealed in such reports. It is largely futile to commission a good independent review, accept it, do the easy things, and then lose its more challenging recommendations in the long grass.

The Church must stop treating independent reviews like London buses – no need to board because another one will be along soon. The risk of this happening is all the greater when later reports are conducted by loyal church members who reach more anodyne conclusions.

In 2018 the Church commissioned a distinguished senior social worker, Sir Roger Singleton, to report on its 2007-2009 Past Cases Review. Inconsistencies in the way it was conducted had become apparent.

The Singleton Report concluded that the Past Cases Review was deeply flawed. Seven dioceses were said to have conducted it so shoddily that the work would need to be done again. Worst of all in some ways, a major attempt had been made by National Church leaders to reduce the number of problematic files. One diocese reported figures well over 100 that were reduced, by narrowing criteria, to just over 30. In the event this figure was reduced to 2.

Thus the Past Cases Review ended up reporting a national state of affairs that would bamboozle Alice in Wonderland – whereas a similar exercise had revealed 2500 past cases in the Methodist Church, and over 1500 in the United Reformed Church, the very much larger Church of England only had 13. *Private Eye* reacted to these figures with incredulity. The Singleton report did not tell the story in such direct terms. It implied there had been problems, but simply concluded it had found no evidence of a systematic attempt to mislead the public.

The evidence, in fact, led to precisely the opposite conclusion – that what had been attempted was obviously a systematic attempt to mislead the public by under-reporting the numbers. No one has yet been held accountable for this.

There is one other glaring hole in the Past Cases Review that affects its validity. It was commissioned following the case of an organist at Farnborough in Surrey. After dealing with clergy records, a second phase could have taken serious steps to elicit disclosures from the public of abuse by Church office holders, volunteers and lay workers who do not have blue files. This glaring weakness remains, and the Church of England cannot claim its Past Cases Review, even if it had been conducted honestly, meets the need it was designed to address in the first place.

Peter Ball's criminal abuse of young people has been much reviewed. The full IICSA hearings of 2018 showed how a succession of previous reviews had failed to get to the heart of the matter. All past cases reviews can only be credible to the extent they are independent. Some good work has been done, but there is further to go for the Church to regain credibility in this area.

Standards of pastoral response to survivors are vastly variable. The problems arising from a lack of independence are compounded by the structure of the Church of England. 42 dioceses run up to 42 different ways of responding to human need. People's experience is even more fragmented where a case straddles more than one diocese. There is a need to stop the current postcode lottery.

One simple reform that would improve matters would be for records to be electronic. At present blue files are usually held as paper records by individual dioceses. If more than one diocese is involved, access to information becomes haphazard and chaotic. If blue files were scanned and held centrally, with appropriate access protocols, critical information would always be available to anyone who needed it, whichever diocese they were in.

Each diocese operates, in fact, as something of a one-man fiefdom. Bishops have a theoretical duty to have regard to Church safeguarding policy, but if they don't nothing seems to happen. One bishop, for example, simply decided he would conduct the supposedly professional past cases review of his own files. This bizarre behaviour did not apparently elicit any response from anyone when it was reported in the Singleton review.

Diocesan Safeguarding Advisors are employees of the bishops whose safeguarding practice they are supposed to monitor and mandate. However professionally competent they may be, they can never be seen as truly independent of their employers.

Again and again, consideration of the Church's failure to live up to its noble ideals comes down to issues of Independence. Audit, risk assessment and case review, have sometimes been conducted well, but we cannot yet say with confidence that the highest standards are consistently being met.

More attention, however, will need to be given to four less developed areas of work for which independence is vital. Accompaniment, Restoration and Redress, Whistleblowing and Clergy Discipline – these call for more radical reform.

4. Accompaniment

In the 1930s the RAF became aware of the kind of burns casualties that might be suffered in a modern war. Various units were set up around the country that swung into action in 1939. The most effective, by a long way, was a hospital in East Grinstead. Its director, Archibald MacIndoe was a plastic surgeon from New Zealand. Some found his practice unorthodox. He allowed his patients beer in hospital, and worked hard to harness any shred of positivity in the ward as a resource for healing. He addressed the social isolation of men with extreme disfigurement by encouraging locals to support the patients and invite them into their homes. He made East Grinstead 'the Town that did not stare'. His patients formed themselves into the 'Guinea Pig Club' and made their distinguished surgeon an honorary member. They became experts in their own care.

Survivor groups like MACSAS have formed, but the Church finds it very difficult to trust them to do their work. It fails to recognise the body of expertise and wisdom amongst them. One project, 'Safe Spaces' has stumbled through over five years of pilots, initiatives and attempted reboots. Funding is in place, but control issues have held it back at every turn.

How would it be if the Church took the same approach as McIndoe to those it has damaged? It is, after all, fundamentally a pastoral organisation. Being there for needy people is what the Church is supposed to do best. This alone might lead people to hope that the pastoral care of people who have been damaged in church would be good.

The local church often gets on with its pastoral work in an unassuming way. There are surely many people who have found hope and healing in their parish church.

For others, however, especially those who have had complex dealings with the national Church, the story seems very different. Survivor after survivor speaks of the utter emotional desert that they experience once they have disclosed to a church official. Not only is there often a deafening silence, but anyone who is at all articulate in expressing their needs soon feels themselves to have been cast as a problem or, even worse, seen as the enemy.

One model for understanding interactions between hurt people is the drama triangle. Transactional Analysis calls this a game of 'Victim, Rescuer, Persecutor.' There are three chairs, V, R and P. The Victim appeals for help to the Rescuer who kindly moves into the 'R' chair. But soon enough the demands of the Victim on the rescuer mount to a point at which the Victim moves into the Persecutor's Chair and the Rescuer over to the Victim's. This becomes a fruitless game of musical chairs which can turn highly toxic. It can go on until somebody deliberately gets up and leaves the triangle.

Of course, people who have been harmed need rescue. Help may be possible, but a Drama Triangle will make things much worse. If the Transactional Analysis 'VRP' game is going on, the Church, faced by unwelcome and potentially large demands that it fears it cannot meet, will soon feel itself to be a victim. It will thus readily start persecuting the person it was originally trying to help, without (for this is the nature of games) any awareness of what is actually going on. A wise accompanier is needed to stand outside the triangle and help Victim and Rescuer work together in a self-aware and fruitful way.

The Church sends out encouraging pastoral messages. Repeatedly it claims its response will be survivor led and put their needs first. One survivor, Jo Kind, writing in the *Church Times* entitled her piece: 'I survived the abuse, but I'm struggling with the response.' Another survivor, Josie Stein, has termed this process 're-abuse.'

It is not an uncommon experience. Mark (1) made multiple efforts to disclose, including to his own mother. Far from being attentive to Mark's pain, Desmond the Cathedral Dean consoles a worried bishop's staff with his icy advice that:

The best way to deal with these people is ignore them. They always go away in the end.

This telltale sentence is deeply shocking. It reveals zero genuine concern for the survivor. Desmond's words are very revealing, not only of his attitude, but that of the people in the room when he said it. Plainly the culture of the senior staff team accepts and reinforces dereliction of duty. This culture, privately hostile to survivors, is reinforced and normalised every time such comments are made. It is in many ways a survivor's worst nightmare – an intentional wall of silence.

Blanking can occur at any stage after disclosure. The initial response can easily be dominated by the anxiety of the person receiving the disclosure. There is a huge temptation to put the matter into the 'too difficult' box . Sometimes there is genuine warmth and empathy, but this tends to dissipate once the lawyers and insurers have been consulted.

What survivors frequently experience are fine disembodied words, where they hoped for pastoral care. In November 2014 Archbishop Justin Welby opened his heart about abuse in the Church of England to the General Synod:

> We are not seeking to say how devastatingly, appallingly, atrociously sorry we are for the great failure there has been, for our own sakes, for our own flourishings, for the protection of the Church. We are doing it because we are called to live in the justice of God, and we will each answer to him for our failings in these areas.

This noble statement fails to take any moral responsibility for the plight of survivors. His speech considers this a matter of being answerable to God. It is, but he seems, maybe unwittingly, to be saying, 'I am accountable to God, *not* you.' This defies the logic of the Incarnation, where the Word becomes flesh not the other way round. The Christian's highest aspiration is, as Malcolm Guite says of all saints,

To see the ones beside us, face to face,
As living icons, sacraments of grace.

(*Church Times,* 16 November 2018)

The just and ethical approach to others would be 'I am accountable to God *through* you.' Genuine compassion that changes and heals people has to be embodied.

Mark (1) was abused, and disclosed the fact, but could not get any traction thereafter. A companion for the road ahead, better still for him and Anita, would have made a real difference. When the hierarchy closed ranks, he would have had support. He would have been helped to understand the pressure his abuse put on his marriage. An accompanier could even, perhaps, have given him the courage not to give up and allow his case to lapse. As it was, he lost his marriage for lack of support. An ideal companion would have been genuinely independent but would have understood the Church and its systems well enough to ensure he was never bewildered or isolated within the Church's labyrinthine processes.

Most Christians instinctively respond to disclosures with a genuine pastoral heart. It is therefore disabling to them, as well as cruel and destructive, if their lawyers or insurers forbid them from getting pastorally involved with survivors.

This is what happened to 'Survivor B,' according to the Elliott Review:

> The withdrawal of pastoral support to a survivor to avoid financial liability, is unacceptable practice from a safeguarding perspective and contrasts sharply with the stated principles upon which all Church actions are meant to be based. It is not in keeping with *Responding Well* and carries with it significant potential risk to vulnerable survivors of abuse.
>
> If the Church is unable to accept the principles that it has

said that it has adopted, it would be important for it to state this. It has committed itself to the provision of 'informed pastoral care and support to anyone who has suffered abuse'. It has to find a way of delivering this which does not exacerbate further the tension between good safeguarding practice and financial liability.

Significantly, those involved in providing a pastoral service to B from within the Church, all expressed their concern about this direction that they were given. It grated with them and they felt unhappy about it. However, that unhappiness did not reach a sufficiently high level to cause them to openly question it or to reject it.

Ian Elliott's recommendations were accepted by the Church and some months later Sarah Mullaly, then Bishop of Crediton, issued the following guidelines for the way the Church responds pastorally to disclosures:

i   All advice received by agents employed by the Church, should be referenced against the stated policies of the Church before it is followed. Emphasis should be placed on ensuring that financial considerations are not given a priority that conflicts with the pastoral aims of the Church when engaging with survivors of abuse.

ii   The Church should seek to create written down guidance with regard to how it will respond to claims for compensation from survivors. This guidance should be shared with survivors from an early juncture in the process. Every effort should be made to avoid an adversarial approach, placing emphasis on the provision of financial compensation as an aid to healing and closure for the survivor.

iii   A first response to a survivor of abuse within the Church should be the issuing of an apology.

Church officials should always pay heed to this guidance. The Compensation Act 2006 Section 2 provides that

> An apology, an offer of treatment or other redress, shall not of itself amount to an admission of negligence or breach of statutory duty.

No compassionate person should fear that a heartfelt apology will create any liability.

Since the events examined in the Elliott Review, Insurers have undertaken further work. Ecclesiastical Insurance has now drawn up guidelines for good practice in collaboration with a survivor, Julie Macfarlane. These are ahead of the insurance industry in general, for example by agreeing not to use time limitation clauses to evade any responsibility to meet claims. In the light of these MACSAS advises:

> There is no reason that pastoral care for church members should be affected by the making of a claim. While your lawyer and EIG will be corresponding about the progress of your claim, your own church can and should continue '...to support the claimant through the provision of pastoral care'.

Shockingly, many survivors still experience responses that fall short of this standard. Financial considerations are easily given priority, along with concern for the Church's image and legal niceties. There is often minimal communication with the survivor. Any apologies feel formulaic.

A simple scheme to accompany survivors would be transformative. After what can be many, many years of carrying a great pain alone, the experience of being taken seriously, listened to, given time and respect, is very powerful. It is often healing in itself. Most pastors have sat with someone who told their story and found doing that, in itself, hugely helpful. They have probably not done anything very wise or special. Simply being in the room with a survivor and believing in them can make a world of difference.

Many survivors do not want the Church involved in any way in addressing their need. This is more than understandable. As one survivor once said to a bishop who was trying to be helpful, 'Why should I want a lift home from the person who's just mugged me?'

Some survivors do want help from counsellors, and fondly believe the Church might know of someone who could help people it has damaged. They are baffled if it doesn't.

This does not build confidence in the Church as a pastoral organisation. At the very least the Church could maintain a database of professional counsellors, with profiles and introductory information, to help people if they want it. The Church needs be realistic about the costs and pace of psychotherapeutic work. The £500 at which one rape survivor's counselling budget was capped is ridiculous and offensive.

Accompaniment is relational work. Its quality and effectiveness come from the skill and experience of the people concerned.

There is sometimes confusion around the accompanier's role, with a notion that their work is 'just pastoral,' so almost anyone could do it.

One Diocesan Safeguarding Advisor decided to set up a listening scheme for survivors. He thought he could simply advertise for volunteers in church notice sheets with almost no screening. If the use of enthusiastic amateurs caused any ructions he was willing to smooth them out personally. This approach is, as kindly as can be said, naïve.

Good accompaniment is a headline service that requires awareness, experience, versatility and skill. The most important person in the process is the first one the complainant sees. This first responder establishes a primary relationship with them and sets the tone with a competent person-centered approach. Reabuse is a constant hazard. A poor response at this initial stage can cause almost irredeemable harm and pain.

There are good models of what accompaniment could look like. Since 2011 the state has trained 'Independent Domestic Violence Advisors.' Back in the 1980s the Church established a system of 'Bishop's Visitors.' Their role was to accompany clergy wives after marital breakdown, and ensure the Church did not close ranks behind their husbands. Things have not always worked out well in practice, partly because of a lack of central investment and co-ordination for their work, but the model is there. It could be developed and applied to help survivors of all kinds of abuse.

Things are moving in this direction. In 2017 the Church issued fresh 'Gold Standard' Practice Guidance to support survivors. Most of these guidelines are common sense, rooted in social work practice:

1.14 Support Person
A support person will be offered to all victims/survivors.

The support person may be an authorised listener specifically trained to hold this role or in appropriate cases a Bishop's Visitor. A member of clergy or a holder of the bishop's license may be among those able to undertake this role as they are already trained in pastoral care – they will, however, still be required to undertake further specific training to hold this role.

Victims/survivors who are children or young people will require specialist support; under advice from Children's Service.

The particular role the support person plays must be agreed in consultation with the victim/survivor. The support person, provided the victim/survivor agrees, could be responsible for the following matters:

- Liaising with the statutory agencies;
- Listening to and representing the victim/survivor's pastoral needs;
- Identifying any therapeutic or other needs the victim/survivor may have, and offering choices as how these may be best met;
- Listening to and representing the victim/survivor's views during the management of the safeguarding concern or allegation;
- Recording any meetings or contact they have with the victim/survivor.

The support person will not be responsible for managing the case and will pass on written records to the DSA.

The support person is NOT the confidant of the victim/survivor. They must be bound by a responsibility to disclose to the appropriate authorities (e.g. the Police, DSA, etc.) where:

- Others are at risk of harm
- The victim/survivor makes disclosures of intentions to hurt themselves.

The support person will NOT attend core group meetings.

The last provision gives the game away about the purpose of core groups. The only constant in the membership of many of them seems to have been a lawyer who works for a firm specialising in image management. This last fact in itself feeds a widespread suspicion by survivors that the groups are not constituted to serve their best interests, but rather to help the Church save face. Ironically, the more senior church leaders focus obsessional efforts on reputation management, the lower the Church's reputation sinks.

There are plenty of good intentions and fine words, but

many find little has changed since Ian Elliott's devastating critique of the gap between them and survivor experience. This calls for a fundamental change of heart that is willing to set the needs of the victim above those of the institution. Realigning these priorities will promote the long-term well-being of the Church as well as survivors.

5. Restoration and Redress

Complete restoration empowers victims to become survivors who are replenished, productive and vibrant participants in the community. (Kudakwashe Nyakudya)

Many survivors are brave and resourceful people who undergo extreme pain and hardship at the Church's hands. They find themselves re-traumatised, sometimes homeless and unemployable. Their pain is exacerbated when they have to battle with Church authorities for recognition and redress. What they have suffered calls for more than financial compensation. Survivors need practical support and assistance.

Active clergy and those with whom they work could be much better protected if they were obliged to carry proper professional liability insurance. It would help them to take seriously the potential for damage in their work. It would also provide a measure of the scale of the problem. As with other professions proper indemnity cover could be withdrawn from those who pose an enhanced risk, in order to protect the public. All this would increase public trust in the church.

In terms of safeguarding process the Church has put a lot of new investment into handbooks, protocols, and staff. Insurers can handle much of the financial aspect. These things matter, but are far from the whole story. All too often payouts are the end, not the beginning, of a pastoral relationship.

The Church has a lead or follow choice. When all is said and done, the Church instructs its lawyers, image managers, and insurers, not the other way round. It should not outsource its pastoral responsibility to them.

All over the world, Churches are groaning under the weight of multiple apologies. The Pope, the Archbishop of Canterbury, endless other senior clerics, issue a seemingly endless stream of tearstained statements expressing their Churches' sorrow and guilt.

And yet … nothing changes.

When the Pope visited Ireland in August 2018, he met survivors who expressed frustration at the glacial pace of change. Neither the whole system nor errant individuals appeared to have been held to account. Nothing measurable was happening to indicate a fundamental change in culture.

The most concrete evidence of contrition would be full and just redress. This would involve the Church recognising the scope of the damage done to a person's whole life. It would then work with the survivor to put together a package driven by, and proportionate to, their need, not the Church budget. It would prioritise the people it has harmed instead of prioritising its image. When serious attention is not paid to doing this the stakes are potentially catastrophic, not only for survivors but for churches.

On 31 May 2018 an agreement was reached after years of dispute between the Roman Catholic Archdiocese of St Paul and Minneapolis and 450 clergy abuse survivors. The payout amounted to $210 million, divided between the archdiocese ($40m) and its insurers ($170m). Archbishop Bernard Hebda, announced the settlement:

> I recognise that the abuse stole so much from you – your childhood, your innocence, your safety, your ability to trust, and in many cases your faith … Relationships with family

and friends, relationships in your parishes and communities were harmed, lives were forever changed. The church let you down. I am very sorry.

Eighteen Catholic dioceses and religious orders in the USA have had to file for bankruptcy. The Archdiocese of St Paul and Minneapolis is likely to become the nineteenth.

As yet there have been no payouts on this scale in the United Kingdom, but the prospect of a trend in this direction may well await the Church of England. It is known among survivors that at one stage the Church scoped a figure of £220m as a contingency fund for uninsured costs arising from past safeguarding failures. It looks as though this sensible provision has evaporated. Survivors see multimillion pound projects being funded by the central Church, whilst they struggle to get basic projects like the SCIE survivor survey or counselling for people like Jennifer (12) funded.

Jennifer's life was torn apart by abuse she suffered in church. She was offered £10,000 as an *ex-gratia* payment then a paltry £500 for counselling. Many people will feel this level of redress, arrived at with little reference to the person's actual needs, is insulting.

It simply is not true that the hands of the bishops are tied. Their job is to work out the right thing to do and then employ their insurers and lawyers to deliver the moral good. It is the only way to avoid a charge of hypocrisy. They have to deliver on what they say.

To do this, they need to begin with the question: 'What does this person need to get peace of mind and create a future for themselves in which they could flourish?' If the starting point is either 'what can we afford?' or 'we have to remember that this is a very damaged person,' then, in Good Samaritan terms, they will be seen to have 'passed by on the other side.'

Survivors say the Church's response to them is piecemeal. Every diocese is autonomous and has developed its own safeguarding culture. Some respond to survivors better than others. When cases straddle more than one diocese, as many do, they are handled by the last one in the line. This is not necessarily the one with the greatest knowledge or the one that carries the actual responsibility. This fact, in itself, shows the need for a national body with the authority to deliver consistently within an overall redress framework.

This needs to apply across the board. It must be driven by the needs of each survivor. The effects of abuse and a plan to heal and move forward in life should be developed and agreed with the person concerned, by a specialist team taking into account four dimensions:

- Psychological harm and the ongoing support needed
- Life chances changed by the abuse, and possibilities for retraining, coaching and career support
- Financial hardship, including loss of income and lack of pension provision
- Spiritual deficit. If the survivor so wishes a spiritual friend could help detoxify faith as a resource for living.

The cost of doing this would vary according to the needs of each individual. Insurers should do their work and apply standard scales of compensation fairly and equally. As they close their files on a case, as they must, the Church needs to step up its pastoral response to the survivor. It should not hand over an insurance cheque and then sign off, feeling its conscience is now clear.

Large costs should not be beyond the resources of the Church of England, which has deep coffers. Over the years the Church has squirrelled away billions of pounds for a rainy day. Today it is raining very hard and those resources need to be drawn down.

One thing is certain. The most costly option is doing nothing. That cost will be paid in people as well as money. In the face of abuse, cover up, lying and silence, people vote with their feet.

In August 2018 the Pope's visit to Ireland put into figures the catastrophic consequences of abuse and poor institutional response, cover-up and injustice to victims. In 1979 Pope John Paul II celebrated a public outdoor Mass with 1,250,000 people. On Sunday 26 August 2018 Pope Francis celebrated Mass in the same location for 250,000. 80% of Irish Catholics had apparently walked away from his Church. The Church of England is standing right at the edge of the same cliff.

The effect of doing the right thing could be transformational. Had someone independent, with no investment in the size of the settlement, asked Jennifer (12) the simple question 'How can we help?' her life might have stood a chance of being re-built. This would have meant funding proper counselling, life coaching, educational courses, transitional housing: any number of possibilities appropriate for her.

Next day, he took out two denarii and handed them to the innkeeper and said, 'Look after him, and on my way back I will make good any extra expense.'

A Church acting like the Good Samaritan would have paid more attention to the needs of the survivor than its own budget.

6. Whistle-blowing policy
UK law (Public Interest Disclosure Act 1998 Section 23) promises whistleblowers protection. The reason for this is that it is impossible to make significant improvements to any service if the law sides with those who wish to cover up when things go wrong.

In this area, though, the Church has various get-out-of-jail-free cards. The employment status of clergy is not entirely clear. The act does not apply to volunteers, and, above all, the Church has no whistleblowing policy. This helps to ensure that what goes on in church stays in church. Knowledge of what has gone wrong is kept within the purple circle. Thus change is held at bay, and whistleblowers have, effectively, no protection.

A healthy society depends on the courage and honesty of people who are prepared to report abuse. Without them the abuser can, and usually does, continue to cause grievous harm. Some survivors are unable to speak about their experience until decades later. That is why effective safeguarding training must include how to notice a possible anomaly which the abused probably cannot themselves report.

Mark (1) complained to his parish priest about the way Father Ian had abused him. This set in train a complex chain reaction of senior ecclesiastics having quiet words, speculating, talking to their lawyers, drawing up statements, and engaging in sundry kinds of damage limitation. Mark experienced no more than the offer of a spiritual director from his vicar, and then silence for more than ten years. Had Father Ian not been promoted to be a bishop this might have lasted to the grave.

No institution likes to hear about its failures. Because the heart of the Church is to be good news it has an almost existential problem when it is experienced as bad news. All survivors are trying to do is describe what happened, and its impact on their lives. The Church can encode this, however, as a wholesale attack. It threatens the sense of being a force for good in the world that is an important part of its identity.

If the survivor seeking justice and redress doesn't give up, this will almost inevitably trigger more defensive behaviour. The Church says it wants to help the survivor and prioritise their interests. Deep down, however, it is affronted by their accusations, and desperately wants them to go away.

No wonder that whistleblowing requires a special sort of courage. Within Church circles it often seems like betrayal. It means telling senior people what they don't want to know about their institution and themselves. It usually involves challenging people in roles that are enmeshed in their understanding of God himself and thus seem beyond question.

The accusation of betrayal is multi-layered.

First, there is the distaste for the idea of 'doing dirty washing in public.' There is huge pressure just to have a quiet word with someone who, like as not, will respond: 'leave it with me.' As Mark (1) struggled to get his story taken seriously, this happened again and again.

Second, there is a risk of spiritual blackmail.

> 'Of course the church is never going to be perfect this side of heaven, but you must not do anything to undermine the greater project of God's mission.'

This can be very powerful, but misses the point. There *is* no mission if it is based on secrecy and cover-up. What price the Church of God if truth and justice are not its foundations?

Third, there is the power of the tribe. An Evangelical ordinand blew the whistle on a more senior Evangelical and felt her card had been marked by her friends in a way that would harm her career. Similar dynamics can be found among all ecclesiastical tribes.

The story of Lucy (15) highlights this issue. As an ordinand she was vulnerable in many ways. At the beginning of her career she probably felt at the mercy of her Diocesan Director of Ordinands and College Principal. She needed a full response to her disclosure and also protection in terms of her career. In fact both those authority figures made it up as they went along. They talked her out of making a formal complaint to the police, choosing instead to deal with it in-house. The failure of the system to protect her privacy meant that her cohort of students would always know that she had made a complaint against 'one of them'.

Mandatory reporting and a whistleblowing policy would have protected Lucy. Whistle blowers would no longer find themselves exposed. It would become a professional and legal duty for them to flag up their concerns. This would depersonalise their decision to speak out.

Sadly, things rarely end well for whistleblowers anywhere. Many NHS careers have been wrecked or changed by it. In *The Times* (25 August 2018) the Health Editor Chris Smyth reports on the case of Marjan Jahangiri:

> A leading heart surgeon was posted a dead animal and a decapitated doll as part of a 'campaign of bullying and harassment' after she raised concerns about unsafe care.

One witness in a recent Clergy Discipline Measure case found herself in Lucy's situation (15). The person against whom she was complaining was much loved and respected. She was one of several women making complaints and felt especially vulnerable to the tribal consequences of her disclosure. The bishop receiving her disclosure was anxious to reassure her about her position and consulted one of the Church's senior legal officers. His enquiry established that there is simply no whistleblowing policy in the Church of England.

Further experience in preparing CDMs exposes various levels of anxiety, sometimes real fear, in complainants. People are prepared to say things off the record but are too afraid to make a formal complaint for fear of the consequences.

John Ortberg, a former senior pastor at a well-known US Megachurch, describes the vulnerability of whistle blowers there:

> I was approached over four years ago with disturbing information that I did not seek out. Along with others who received this information I directed it to the elders of Willow Creek. The process that followed was, in my view, poorly designed and likely to expose the woman who came forward to grave risks.

Cultures of fear, and lack of care for those with the courage and honesty to come forward, creates something like a Jimmy Savile Syndrome. As the truth about Savile began to emerge a large number of people said that they had always thought he was a bit creepy. It seems everyone suspected he was up to no good. Because almost no-one dared to say, and those who tried to were not taken seriously, Savile went on to abuse many, many more people and cause each one of them a lifetime's worth of pain.

On the eve of the papal visit to Ireland in 2018 prosecutors in the United States published a 1,300 page report into clerical abuse of children in Pennsylvania. Its magnitude was off the scale. More than 1,000 children had been sexually abused by 301 priests over 70 years. One diocesan priest, Father Boniface Ramsey, tried:

> I have blown the whistle for 30 years without getting anywhere.

Although English law theoretically protects whistleblowers, in practice it can only take effect if those responsible take steps to implement it in their organisations.

The NHS, which we have seen still finds it difficult to get this right, has very clear policy to protect whistleblowers:

5.1 The 'Whistle Blowing' Policy is intended to cover serious public interest concerns that fall outside the scope of other procedures. These, as stated in the Act are that in the reasonable belief of the employee, the following matters are either happening now, have happened, or are likely to happen:

- A criminal offence
- The breach of a legal obligation
- A miscarriage of justice
- A danger to the health and safety of an individual
- Damage to the environment
- Deliberate covering up of/failing to report information tending to show any of the above five matters.

The policy goes on to assure the whistle-blower both of their safety, including about employment, and anonymity. Going to the media invalidates that clause.

The ethos of this statement is openness, at least in theory. It carried a strap line at the top:

'If in doubt – raise it.'

There is a very clear process to follow here and it would be straightforward for the Church of England to formulate something similar.

The weakness is not in the policy, but in the hearts of the people who deliver it. NHS staff still get stigmatised and even lose their jobs. There is huge cultural resistance in the Church of England to requiring every diocesan bishop to follow a common policy about anything. Doing this is easily seen as a threat to bishops' autonomy, watering down their power.

Sadly, there are people running the church who would simply rather not know when things go wrong. A good and robust whistleblowing policy is needed to create a proper level of accountability and to set a standard for the way things should be. Policy alone will not solve the problem. Implementation is everything.

English law intends that whistleblowers should be properly protected. The challenges and complexities of actually doing this should not put the Church off trying. Indeed this could be an opportunity to give a lead rather than tagging lamely along behind.

7. Clergy discipline

A cautionary tale

On 4 February 2016 the headteacher of a rural Church of England Primary School reported to their Governors that a Fire Practice had taken place in the school, in compliance with its health and safety policy. She had filled in a Fire Safety form the previous June stating the same. The Custodian was responsible for conducting a weekly test, with a personal evacuation plan in place for the building.

Sadly these reassuring statements were not actually true. Due to pressure of work and the multiple demands heads of small schools experience, the Head had ticked the boxes but not got around to implementing the policy. She then attempted to cover her tracks. This relatively minor and understandable act of dishonesty placed the school at risk.

Eighteen months later the head teacher came before a disciplinary panel of the National College of Teaching and Learning. The hearing took place in public and was recorded. Documents were submitted by all parties who were legally represented. After careful examination of written evidence and personal testimony from the head a finding of fact was recorded. The panel went on to consider on this basis:

> whether the facts of the proved allegations amounted to unacceptable professional conduct and/or conduct that may bring the profession into disrepute.

Applying the relevant professional guidelines it found the alleged behaviour fell significantly short of the standards expected in the teaching profession.

Next, the panel debated whether to recommend the Secretary of State to issue a Prohibition Order. It carefully weighed the public's high expectations of truthfulness, and relevant safety considerations, against the loss to the profession of a gifted and able teacher. She had a previously good history and the panel took into account the professional and personal pressures on her at the time. Nobody had in fact been harmed. There was no evidence of a reckless attitude and no risk of repetition. This was an isolated incident in a long and successful career. The Head had demonstrated genuine insight and remorse. She had complied fully with the NCTL proceedings.

All things considered, after four closely argued pages, the panel decided to recommend:

> an indefinite Prohibition Order barring the Head from work in any school, sixth form college, relevant youth accommodation or children's home in England.

She was given permission to apply for the order to be set aside after two years. She was reminded she had a right of appeal to the Queen's Bench Division of the High Court within 28 days of receiving the order.

This case is one of many arising from the work of 506,400 teachers in England. It shows how the profession deals with safeguarding failures by those in authority. It is not a particularly bad case, and although it came fully into the public domain there is no reason why the Head should not find another job after two years and a risk assessment. Justice was done, and seen to be done. The Head, were she to return to teaching, might, however, have to explain her offence and what she had done about it.

Parson's Pleasure?

At present, the Church of England deals with such matters differently. Its disciplinary system is experienced by many survivors as self-protective and inconsistent.

The system contains a high degree of discretion. Complainants often experience dilatory performance in operating the machinery, and a culture of excessive secrecy. It is also said that some diocesan bishops use the CDM system far more than others.

After 15 years of operation, very few people have a good word to say for the Clergy Discipline Measure. Attention to its deficiencies is urgently needed. But how? What would progress look like and achieve? What snags might there be in developing it?

The Hot Stove Rule

One model approach to professional discipline in the business world has stood the test of time for over fifty years. The 'Hot Stove Rule' is attributed to Douglas McGregor. When you touch a hot stove you burn your hand immediately, in a way that is predictable, the same for anyone, and impersonal. Therefore any disciplinary system will cause resentment and will not work unless it succeeds at four tasks:

- **Finding out what actually happened.** Before anything else, the facts will be fully investigated and established on the balance of probabilities. Staff will be fully involved in this process, and accompanied and represented appropriately.
- **Communicating expectations to everyone to whom they apply.** Businesses will be clear and transparent about policies, rules and regulations from induction on,

so that people cannot say they did not know what would happen if they transgressed.

- **Achieving consistency – justice for all to whom it applies.**
  Whatever their position in the company, policies are applied fairly and equally.
- **Directing action on the basis of the act, not the person.**
  It should never be undertaken arbitrarily or at the discretion of the individual manager.

When 'Hot Stove' principles are followed staff members know that, before anything else happens, care will be taken to establish the facts. They will be treated exactly as anyone else in the organisation would have been, the basis of the truth revealed by careful investigation. This will be done in as timely a way as possible. This will enable the organisation to close its file and for everybody, including other staff members, to learn from what has gone wrong.

The NCTL enquiry above began by considering the facts fully and in detail. Everyone was represented. A statement of agreed facts was drawn up, and everything else determined on the balance of probabilities.

This was done before any negotiation about penalties and mitigating factors. These two phases were dealt with separately. The penalty was carefully formulated according to procedures and principles about which any head should have known at the time of the offence.

The whole process took 30 months. All disciplinary proceedings seem unsatisfactorily long. They need notice periods and time to prepare for a full and fair hearing. By comparison the same period in a recent CDM case was 51 months, with process wobbles all along the way. In school, all proceedings were put into the public domain. Therefore no other head, tempted to be economical with the truth about fire drills, should be in any doubt as to the professional consequences. Broadly speaking, NCTL applied discipline to this teacher according to 'hot stove' principles.

Clergy Discipline Measure – Impact

For the past 15 years the only lawful apparatus to uphold professional standards among the clergy has been the Clergy Discipline Measure, 2003.

Many complainants like Linda (8), including abuse survivors, find trying to use it at best frustrating, at worst outrageously arbitrary and unjust.

Many respondents, like Jane (11), have found it burdensome, capricious, and emotionally destructive.

Few bishops have much good to say of it. One CDM against a bishop was dismissed recently, partly on the grounds that a diocesan bishop could not be expected to understand the workings of the measure. If bishops, who are the lynchpins of the system, can't be expected to understand it, what chance the public?

Many lawyers who operate the machinery are fully aware of its shortcomings. They too are frustrated by their inability to do anything to improve it. There are occasional reviews, but recommendations, even from senior church lawyers, seem to be studiously ignored as unnecessary or too expensive to implement. People are told the bother of getting new legislation through the General Synod would be prohibitive, with no appetite for change there. Anecdotally, however, it seems many synod members are frustrated, too, whenever the dense fog of secrecy about CDM lifts sufficiently to reveal fragmentary facts about the present shambles.

The Church appears to believe that maintaining basic professional standards is a luxury it cannot afford. It seems everything is done on the cheap. The result is the worst of all worlds. A tiny minority of dangerous clergy make a monkey of the whole system, whilst the majority of good and decent clergy are terrified of its rumoured capriciousness and arbitrariness.

Since 1987 the Society of Mary and Martha has provided a sanctuary for clergy of all denominations. In 2002 it produced *Affirmation and Accountability*, a ground-breaking report to help Churches understand how to support clergy and hold them truly accountable. The report was based on the Society's extensive experience of working with people trying to pick up the pieces after collapse or burnout in ministry.

In 2018 SMM commissioned a new research project called *What is wrong with CDM?*

It is becoming clear that there are serious problems with the Church of England's Clergy Discipline Measure (CDM). Recurring themes and issues are highlighted by the hundreds of Anglican clergy using The Hub.

- Clergy are ensnared in a process in which they are much more vulnerable than professionals in any other discipline and which has no ombudsman oversight.
- Bishops are fundamentally compromised by being asked to fulfil mutually incompatible roles of Investigator, Prosecutor, Judge and Pastor.
- Archdeacons dread being sucked into the mire of administering the process.
- Clergy families unfairly suffer the detriment of their own home, community and finances.
- Even complainants seldom get the satisfaction they seek.

A tiny minority of bullies have been given license to make everyone's life a misery. The quality of pastoral and working relationships between clergy and senior staff are being eroded with invidious results. At every level, time, energy and money are being drained. There are no winners. Anecdotal evidence is all we can work with because data collection is completely inadequate on both process and outcomes. Anecdotal evidence includes:

- Delays in processing cases leave people in limbo for many months or even years.
- Serious impacts on short and long-term mental health – especially anxiety and depression.
- Ruinous costs from legal fees when specialist ecclesiastical lawyers are needed for which the church's legal aid does not provide full indemnity.
- Leaving ministry because of inadequate support to either rehabilitate in the parish or move to a new post.
- A legacy of poor physical and mental health and marital relationship stress.

The Clergy Discipline Measure, according to those who help its casualties pick up the pieces after it has been used, has a vastly negative human impact. It is hard for anyone who lives with these daily realities to come to any other conclusion.

But does it work?

Some collateral damage could be seen as necessary to deter wrongdoing and protect the public. So how effective is the CDM? What does it actually achieve? How does it, as it is experienced, stack up in terms of Douglas McGregor's 'Hot Stove' model?

The hot stove actually exists. Therefore the first task of all 'hot stove' disciplinary practice is establishing exactly what happened.

One common theme of survivor CDM experience

is slackness about investigating the facts. Gossip and innuendo abound in the church, and much business has customarily been done on an unrecorded discretionary basis. Concern about data protection has sometimes led to files being weeded, making it even more difficult to get at the truth of what actually happened. In Mark's case (1) all the communication lines between the people to whom he reported were scrambled or confused. People relied on bumping into colleagues, and as memory faded, made inaccurate assumptions about what was alleged and on what grounds. Thus Mark was turned from a server into a choirboy without anybody noticing.

Establishing the facts forensically has to be the foundation of any disciplinary system not an afterthought. It is vastly draining and frustrating to survivors when they have to grind the truth out of Church authorities, kicking and screaming, line by line. They often, understandably, hear:

> 'We will only be willing to say anything about this after the next inquiry.'

as code for:

> 'We would rather wait and see what someone else manages to unearth about us and respond to that than deal seriously with your situation now.'

The Clergy Discipline Measure provides, sensibly, that if a cleric is convicted of a crime there is a fast track procedure for putting them on a caution list. The vast majority of CDM tribunals, however, arise from gross professional misconduct that is not criminal. This includes dishonesty, like lying about a fire practice, drunkenness or adultery.

We have seen that 'hot stove' disciplinary systems

enable organisations to close the file, learn from mistakes and move on.

The vast majority of CDM complaints are handled in a way which makes this outcome intellectually impossible. A complaint is received, say, of adultery. This is followed by CDM preliminaries, with the marshalling of witnesses and their evidence. At this point the lawyer for the accused may well advise their client that the game is up, so the best option would be to resign with a secret agreement. That way nobody will ever know that anything went wrong (except the witnesses) and the Church can move on in a way that's economical and saves embarrassment.

You could say everybody wins, but this wouldn't be the case. The witnesses are left with a deep sense of injustice because something very wrong has happened, and the Church has been more concerned to cover it up and save face than to learn from it. Many complainants end up thinking the CDM is rotten, corrupt and self-serving, mainly because it is. A negotiated solution has been allowed before anyone bothered to establish the facts. The truth matters. Post-apartheid South African experience demonstrates that truth is the foundation of reconciliation.

In CDM proceedings the truth is rarely investigated. Even when it is, a non-disclosure agreement may well keep it safely under the carpet. This problem is especially acute if, as is often the case, a gagging order is imposed before there has been a finding of fact.

This enables the offender to kid themselves about what has happened, carry on and apply for other similar jobs. These will theoretically be outside the Church if the offender has been caution listed. The truth about that, however, is that circulating the list is such a low priority at Lambeth Palace that whole years have gone by recently without it happening. This fact, in itself, makes the list useless as an aid to safe recruitment.

There must be, as there have always been, clergy who are such menaces they should be struck off, or, as the colourful old phrase has it, 'unfrocked.' Unfortunately the ability to do this is said to have been traded for votes in the House of Clergy to get CDM legislation through the General Synod. Therefore, clergy are probably the only professional group who cannot be 'struck off' whatever they do.

It does not help reduce complainants' frustration and anger that a 'value for money' threshold has recently begun to be applied to complaints. Behaviour like drunkenness, aggression or lying is not usually thought weighty enough to warrant the cost and bother of a tribunal.

Diocesan bishops can only impose penalties at the first stage of CDM, and only with the consent of the respondent. Therefore an honest cleric who has been drunk in church may well own up, accept a conditional deferment (the CDM equivalent of a Police Caution), and be offered help. A dishonest cleric, however, can deny all, safe in the knowledge that the chair of tribunals is unlikely to think it economic to pursue the matter. Thus the CDM penalises the honest cleric and privileges those who game the system. The CDM ends up overcooking trivia, but unable to address serious or psychopathic behaviour.

When no action is taken it hurts victims and witnesses alike:

'So he gets away with it!' said Colin (8). 'Six of one and half a dozen of the other? He doesn't agree he should be punished, so let's not bother! A pastoral solution? What would that be? At long last His Lordship rules – "Boys will be boys!"'

The only response CDM can offer to reports of drunkenness from undertakers, scared parishioners and intimidated witnesses, is that the police could catch the cleric drink driving. Apart from that, nothing can be done. The powers that be may describe such a denouement as 'a pastoral solution.' It is hard to see much pastoral about it. It doesn't solve anything, except, perhaps, the problem of moving the file off the judge's desk. Some pastoral solutions require disciplinary action. Until this problem is taken seriously, the CDM is a charter for wolves in sheep's clothing.

If a case comes down to one person's word against another, this does not inevitably prevent a tribunal from taking a view on the balance of probabilities. A sexual assault may well be far more memorable to the victim than to the perpetrator. By their very nature such incidents usually take place in private. Very few are witnessed by third parties. If lack of outside witnesses is always decisive, tribunals are effectively always going to find against the victim. On the other hand a policy of always believing the accuser would open the way to wrong findings of guilt.

This dilemma was at the heart of the recent senate hearings to confirm Judge Brett Kavanaugh as a Justice of the Supreme Court. Both parties gave passionate and extensive evidence, entirely believable from their point of view, and that of their supporters. Many were left feeling it would never be possible to decide what really happened.

But was this the only possible conclusion? Nathan J. Robinson thinks not:

> The existence of a 'he said, she said' does not mean it's impossible to figure out the truth. It means we have to examine what he said, and what she said, as closely as possible. If both parties speak with passion and clarity, but one of them says many inconsistent, evasive, irrational, and false things, while the other does not, then we actually have a very good indicator of which party is telling the truth. If a man claims to be innocent, but does things – like carefully manipulate words to avoid giving clear answers, or lie about the evidence – that you probably wouldn't do if you were innocent, then testimony alone can substantially change our confidence in who to believe.

The second task of a 'Hot Stove' disciplinary system is to be open about what has happened. Staff members need to know so that they can take note and learn. The public need to know in order to have confidence that justice has been done. They also need to know that the institution can be trusted to deal with serious professional misconduct.

In practice, Clergy Discipline Measure proceedings are exceptionally secretive.

For a start, the way information is handled seems whimsical. A CDM complaint from Brussels in the diocese of Europe in May 2016 (Day) catalogues the respondent's 'conduct unbecoming' in gross detail. This was necessary, we are told, because downloading pornography is not a criminal offence in Belgium. But the report also revealed details about the breakup of the respondent's marriage which would not, in themselves, have been offences in England at the time. This is inconsistent with the way such matters are reported in English CDMs, where a county court finding of 'Unreasonable Behaviour' in a divorce case is not reported in gruesome detail.

It is hard to read this decision without a queasy feeling that something very odd is going on, and far too much information has been given. It is disturbing to think that the tribunal gave no thought to the possible impact on the respondent's children and their friends of all that was published. Teaching Regulation Agency (successor body to the National College of Teaching and Leadership) judgments redact sensitive revelations that could damage a child. Surely the CDM tribunal could have accomplished its purpose whilst still observing a similar discipline?

In fact most CDM proceedings in England are cloaked in a thick fog of secrecy. Fellow clergy and the public know nothing of the existence, let alone the findings, of the vast majority of complaints, because they have been resolved by the diocesan bishop at stage one. This leaves the witnesses in the dark, and means that no one outside the situation will ever learn anything from what has happened.

Administrative suspension is almost never imposed by the Church. Often bishops persuade respondents to withdraw from ministry voluntarily. This is often an attempt to be kind, given how stressful suspension would be. What happens instead, however, is often even more stressful. Without any need to review the position every three months, as with suspension, withdrawals drag on, sometimes for years. This prolongs everything agonisingly and, in itself, almost inevitably fuels speculation and creates waves of gossip in the parish, which can have a lasting impact on the viability of an innocent respondent's ministry.

Refusal to suspend also works as a kind of anti-whistleblowing policy. It can expose members of the public to additional danger. Since only the respondent, bishop, archdeacon and witnesses know that there is anything going on, there is plenty of scope for continued offending and witness intimidation. The fact that suspension is so rare also means that on the very rare occasions it happens it feels, in itself, like a guilty finding. Some clergy have self-harmed and even taken their lives because they felt they had already been judged and found guilty.

Suspension policy needs to change. It has to be done according to clear criteria that are made known to the respondent. There has to be a right of appeal and a requirement for three monthly review and renewal, and these are already provided in the CDM code of practice. Only once administrative suspension ceases to be an extreme measure reserved for the most heinous cases can it be experienced as neutral, and proper space be given for investigation.

The policy of non-suspension also limits the scope of any investigation. In many abuse cases people only come forward to disclose when the perpetrator has been removed from the scene, making it safe for them to do so. Almost no victims of Jimmy Savile felt safe enough to come forward with evidence until he was dead.

Finally, wholesale refusal to suspend imposes on conscientious clergy under investigation, like Jane (11), an obligation to keep things going in the parish as best they can, bearing the burden of being under investigation alone.

A good disciplinary system deters wrongdoers and educates everyone. Only when people who know the hot stove will burn them can they avoid it. Obsessive secrecy surrounding CDM makes it almost impossible for this to happen because nobody knows where lines have been drawn.

A hundred years ago getting into an aeroplane was one of the most dangerous things you could do. It is said more Royal Flying Corps pilots in the First World War were killed by their machines than by the enemy. A hundred years on, flying is one of the safest means of transport. The inherent risks have been mastered and largely overcome by technological advance, informed by a rigorous habit of investigating accidents in minute detail, then applying what has been learnt.

Things are not so in the medical world. Despite best endeavours, investigations of medical accidents and malpractice often feel like cover-ups. Improvement seems stubbornly slow. In June 2018 a committee chaired by Bishop James Jones, produced *Gosport War Memorial Hospital: The Report of the Gosport Independent Panel*. The attitudes and culture it describes resonate with another report from 16 years earlier – *Learning from Bristol: the Report of the Public Inquiry into children's heart surgery at the Bristol Royal Infirmary 1984–1995*. There seems to be a stubbornly persistent pattern of self-reinforcing failure here. People intend to learn but they don't. Old habits die hard and self-replicate. The more bad practice is kept secret, the harder this cycle is to break.

A similar pattern of cyclical failure to learn from past errors can be seen in the gushing stream of apologies coming from senior figures in the Church. One survivor of abuse has said his dealings with the Church felt as though he had strayed into his own personal Groundhog Day.

Child Protection expert Marcus Erooga points out,

> in a safe environment, children and adults feel able to raise concerns about others and to self-report.

From this point of view CDM, in itself, helps create an unsafe environment in which many abusers flourish freely and unchecked.

The third 'hot stove principle' is consistency. Whoever touches the stove gets burnt exactly the same as anyone else.

So hidden is the whole CDM apparatus that there is usually no way of knowing who is involved, let alone the outcome.

It could well be that when the clergy disciplinary system was devised it was not imagined there would ever be a significant number taken out against bishops. In practice, legal professionals say privately that *pro rata* ten times as many CDMs are taken out against bishops as against other clergy. It may be that there are bishops who have indeed experienced disciplinary consequences from having breached safeguarding policy. Nobody knows. Nothing goes to a tribunal. Everything is kept, incestuously, within the purple circle.

As complaints against bishops escalate, absurdity abounds, way beyond anything those who framed the CDM can have envisaged. One archbishop could have to hear a complaint about how his fellow archbishop had handled a particular case. At the same time the other archbishop could be presented with a complaint from the same complainant about how the first one had handled another aspect of the same case. Both respondents would simultaneously be advised by members of the same tiny circle of ecclesiastical lawyers. It's cosy, but inquiring minds will wonder, how can it be justice? For any disciplinary system to work properly, justice must be seen to be done.

To be credible, the whole system requires independence at every level. Those who framed the Clergy Discipline Measure in 2003 contained everything at every stage among bishops and archbishops. This, disastrously, makes a bishop combined judge, investigator, prosecutor and pastor. In the film *Oh, Mr Porter!* (1937), Will Hay, a British comedian, found himself having to be station master, train driver and ticket clerk. Many bishops operating CDM feel like Mr Harbottle in the same film:

> Porter, shunter, signalman, deputy stationmaster when there isn't a stationmaster, which is more often than not.

Running a disciplinary system for the Church of England along these lines has not been a winner.

Unsurprisingly, given the Kafkaesque nature of the CDM procedure, and the dense fog of secrecy in which it is conducted, rumours abound among survivors who have tried to use it. What if a bishop takes out a CDM to neutralise a clergy person who is threatening to take out a CDM against him?

Out of Time rules are often used to suppress cases, all over the world. Because of the Statute of Limitations, Cardinal Theodore McCarrick, former Archbishop of Washington, who was reported to have been a gross serial abuser, will face no state prosecution.

Out of Time rules are especially worrisome to people

caught in a system where procedural advances that should be dealt with in 56 days regularly take the best part of a year and sometimes simply seem to disappear into thin air. Some Out of Time CDM complaints against bishops are perceived to go ahead only if the respondents agree to it. There are certainly incidents where a serious complaint relating to a sustained pattern of behaviour has been thrown out because it was received one day late.

Sluggish procedure is a special problem for people struggling with life-changing memories that have been reawakened by making a disclosure. If an otherwise happily married couple have a row and look back at it a year on, they can easily, assuming all is going well between them, put it in perspective and laugh it off. They remember it, but they don't experience afresh the fury of the moment. If, however, an abusive memory is suppressed, sometimes for decades, rather than dealt with, bringing it back to the surface is very likely to reignite everything. The traumatic memory is re-lived, rather than remembered. Forcing survivors to retell their stories again and again is cruel. The cruelty is compounded if after all this, the whole case remains unresolved.

In Douglas McGregor's terms, the CDM hot stove is a very strange piece of apparatus. It cannot operate with any clarity because most of the time people can't see it. Only the most serious incidences of burning ever get reported. It's impossible to know, often, whether the stove is on, or even there. Incredibly, this stove manages to be hotter for some people than for others. It is hard to think such a stove is fit for purpose.

The only way forward is wholesale reform of the process and legislation to provide a system that is consistent, transparent and effective. This will need to address the basic needs of those whose lives it touches, respondents as well as complainants. It must resolve the position of bishops and assert what they are in canon law – chief pastors of their dioceses.

It is often said among survivors that they need a lawyer to access the system in any meaningful way. A reformed system will provide access to justice for all. It will address the issue of administrative suspension. It will deal with serious professional misconduct purely on the basis of fact, not a desire to save money and save face.

At present everything is dependent on one of 42 individual dioceses, with inadequate provision for cases that straddle more than one. This situation calls for a single national body that transcends individual dioceses.

Jane (11), was terrified by a process she did not understand and could not talk about, whilst keeping everything going in her parish as though nothing was up. Linda and Jason (8)'s other parishioners deserved protection from an overbearing and spiritually abusive pastor. A better process would have offered Jason himself an opportunity to understand how his ministry was impacting others, and to amend it accordingly.

Two final caveats are necessary.

The best system of clergy discipline in the world is no magic bullet. It can only deal with clergy. It does nothing to protect clergy like Malcolm (6) who was bullied by a lay office holder, or lay people like Jennifer (12) who was abused by the organist.

This is a complex problem, but a start could be made in addressing it if it became possible, after due inquiry with a right of appeal, to bar lay people from holding office in the Church.

Finally, a good system to deal with the tiny minority of clergy who abuse others cannot work if everything is done on the cheap. It is in everyone's interest to determine carefully what has happened, including in cases that some might think minor offences like drunkenness, verbal abuse, lying and dishonesty.

A lie about a fire practice was enough to get a Church of England primary school head disqualified from office for two years. This was not because of the lie's enormity on the whole scale of wrongdoing, but because parents have to have confidence in those to whom they entrust their children. Teachers must care enough about safety in school to tell the truth. A Church that cannot be bothered to ensure that those who represent it publicly are trustworthy, undermines the work and reputations of the vast majority of clergy who are honest, hardworking and ethical.

It is high time to return to the holy drawing board with the CDM. Proper reform will be time consuming and expensive, but less so than allowing the present abusive shambles to continue.

6

The Heart of the Matter

In all fields of human endeavour, including the way the Church responds to the fact of abuse within it, Sydney Smith was right:

> It is the greatest of all mistakes to do nothing because you can only do little.

We have identified a number of policy areas in which small incremental steps would help. Attention to these cumulatively could transform survivor experience of the Church. Fine words, however, mean nothing if anyone is left bleeding in the road whilst the Church continues to accumulate policy guidelines with handwringing apologies.

Some people have had positive experiences after reporting damage in church. Simple responsive kindness counts for much. This has often been no more than phone calls, cups of coffee, time and loving attention from people who did not pass by on the other side.

Church officials almost always mean well and often say that blocking is not what they intended. People do not always experience what is intended, however. They experience what they experience, and it is a waste of time to try and negate that by saying it was unintended. It probably was, but saying this will not reconcile them to a radio silence that feels like contempt, defensiveness, mendacity and institutional self-protection.

If we are serious about making the Church the safe place everybody believes it should be, there is, to use George

Herbert's colourful phrase, 'a famous stone that turneth all to gold,' but it is emphatically not apologising.

Everybody is apologising these days, from the Pope down. The fulsome apologies meted out at IICSA became very annoying after a while. One survivor reacted by saying to us:

> I understand the bishop when he says how ashamed this makes him feel, and I'm sorry if this is the worst day of his life, but he needs to know this is not about his feelings. I don't want him to feel bad. I want him to pick up the bloody phone.

Sometimes abuse survivors find help and healing from friends in their own church. Other local reactions, however, can exacerbate abuse, especially when loyalty to a much-loved but abusive leader causes people to close ranks.

Further up the ecclesiastical food chain there is more distance from survivors and, perhaps, a feeling that more is at stake. Those at the top of a hierarchical institution could lead the way in accepting responsibility and co-ordinating good responses. Instead, much of the time they seem too busy or defensive to be in the same room as survivors, let alone help them.

It is natural for those who have been damaged in church to feel they could get somewhere if only senior figures would take them seriously. Yet if, as happened on one notable occasion, it becomes apparent three-quarters of the way through a meeting that the bishop has not even read the papers, what is going on seems an exercise in futility.

There is no reason a senior figure cannot be more responsive. Yet, again and again, getting a human response from on high seems almost impossible. One survivor has said of a long and complex case stretching over many years,

None of this was necessary. If that bishop had just answered the bloody phone, told the truth and said, 'How can I help?' we wouldn't be where we are today.

Picking up the phone and saying, 'How can I help?' is what a Good Samaritan would do. Picking up the phone to the legal team, then hiding behind the guidelines sounds more like what a Levite would do. Prioritising theology and the Church's reputation feels like what a priest would do, passing by on the other side.

The parable of the Good Samaritan commends people who express their theology by responding to real need. The priest and Levite were not, as far as we know, bad at doing their jobs. They probably had the best intentions. Confronted with a wounded traveller, they left the work of responding to someone else.

This does not mean there is no role for lawyers, insurers, social workers and theologians in addressing abuse. But pastoral response is the thing those who have been abused crave. The Church is responsible for behaving like a Church, not an insurance company, law firm or social work department.

This will involve using teams that are professionally diverse. Abraham Maslow said in 1966,

> it is tempting, if the only tool you have is a hammer, to treat everything as if it were a nail.

It is all very well to staff a sub-department at diocesan HQ entirely with social workers. They can make a significant contribution, but cannot do the whole task. This model usually leaves the survivor outside the core group, and voiceless. What its needed is a balanced multidisciplinary approach, where a whole team, working together use a variety of tools, and the purpose is pastoral. The Church's core pastoral work cannot be outsourced or delegated, and without it everything else is worth nothing.

An old tale, told in parish magazines on both sides of the Atlantic since Victorian times, says as much:

> Once upon a time there were four people – Everybody, Somebody, Anybody and Nobody. There was an important job to be done and Everybody was asked to do it. Everybody was sure Somebody would do it. Anybody could have done it, but Nobody did it. Somebody got angry about that because it was Everybody's job. Everybody thought Anybody would do it but Nobody realised that Everybody wouldn't do it. It ended up that Everybody started blaming Somebody just because Nobody did what Anybody could have done.

The Archbishop of Canterbury agrees about whose responsibility it is to follow the Good Samaritan's example. He says responding pastorally and well is the responsibility of everyone at every level:

> The Church of England is committed to the safeguarding, care and nurture of everyone within our church community so that all can flourish in faith and know the love of God.
>
> We all have a responsibility to care for one another, and to keep people safe from harm, and it is especially important that children and vulnerable adults are protected.

The time has come to make these fine words a reality in the lives of those who have been damaged in church.

7

Mark 2

Things didn't have to end the way they did for Mark. A small amount of compassion in action, like the Good Samaritan, would have made a world of difference.

Mark's story could have ended like this:

'Father Ian ruined my life,' Mark said.

'What do you mean?' Anita asked.

That's when everything came tumbling out.

'Why didn't you tell anyone?' she asked.

'I did try,' he said. 'I told Mum what Father Ian made me do, but she was angry with me for making things up.'

'Well, you've got to tell someone now,' said Anita. 'Quite apart from putting things right for you, he could still be a danger to young children.'

By next morning, Mark knew Anita was right.

All he'd wanted was to forget what happened with Father Ian, but now the wound was open again it was a gaping hole in his life. He had to tell someone. Perhaps he could find a way to put it all behind him.

Five years ago Father Ian had become an archdeacon in another diocese. Mark and the scouts had put on much of his leaving do and he was relieved to see the back of him.

He wasn't comfortable about telling a secular counsellor, so he skirted round the subject with her, but next Sunday he went up to Father Robert in the vestry and arranged a time to see him privately at the vicarage.

Mark knew and liked his parish priest and was used to working with him as head server, but it wasn't easy to talk. Being in the vicarage brought back memories and he realised he wasn't as comfortable as he thought he should be being alone in a priest's study. Father Robert was a good listener. He was deeply shocked by what he heard and promised he would seek advice from the bishop. He prayed with Mark, and there was real concern in his voice as he asked whether there was anything else the Church could do to help.

Later that day, Father Robert picked up the phone to Bishop Simon. 'Bishop, my head server has just been to see me to say my predecessor abused him for three years when he was 12.'

'What kind of thing are we talking about?' asked Bishop Simon

'Oral sex when he came to the vicarage for serving practice, and in the vestry.'

'That's awful. I'm so sorry. There are formal things we'll need to do, but how is he? What's his name?'

'Mark. He was very tearful when he told me. It wasn't easy, and I don't know that I've got everything yet. He's a good server, but rather shy. He also helps with the Scouts. He and his parents have been part of our parish for many years. He's just got married to a girl called Anita, who's young, and really loves him. They've become a bit of a poster couple for our parish Mass congregation.'

'It sounds to me as though I need to meet him and then we can get a clearer idea of how to help. I usually work with my colleague and chaplain, Janet. It means there's a woman present, and she can write up and agree a record of our meeting at the time. Please can we arrange a time for us to visit?'

About ten days later Bishop Simon and Janet went to visit Mark at home. Anita was there to support him, but the story was harrowing.

'I'm so very sorry, Mark,' said Bishop Simon. 'To be honest, this really does sound like a police matter. I'll do everything I can to help.'

'You're right, Simon. It was a crime, but I can't bear the thought of having to go through it in court,' said Mark. 'I can remember every detail of what he did to me like it was yesterday, but I can't face talking about it over and over again.'

'I can see that. I don't think I could do it,' said the bishop. 'You'll have to think it through together until you feel ready. If it helps one of us could come with you ... I'll give you a call next week to see how you're getting on. Father Robert seems to be there for you. That said, I can imagine how difficult it must be for you to work with priests after what happened. If you'd prefer to be supported by someone else, please let me know.'

Mark and Anita talked late into the night. Mark didn't feel ready really, but a feeling welled up in him that Father Ian needed to be stopped before he did the same thing to anyone else. He probably had anyway. It didn't bear thinking about. Being listened to and taken seriously had surprised him. But he needed time to think through what to say and when. He explained that to the bishop when he phoned on Wednesday.

The day before, Janet emailed notes of their meeting round to Mark to check everything was properly recorded.

A fortnight later Mark picked up the phone to Jane. 'Please can you tell Bishop Simon I am going to the police. Anita's coming with me. I don't want what happened to me to happen to anyone else. Anyway, it's the right thing to do ...'

Mark and Anita have just celebrated ten years together. They have a five year old son.

8

Empire or Village?

The experience of survivors we know has raised fundamental questions for us, again and again. The first and most obvious, is: *'What sort of God do we actually believe in?'*

The answer to this primary question should be easy for any follower of Christ to answer. God is love. Jesus Christ is the human face of God. The Lord is the God and Father of our Lord Jesus Christ, with whom he is one.

Its implications are more challenging, though. Scripture says that saying we love God whilst ignoring our neighbour is self-deception. If that is true, and, furthermore, the acid test of the Church's authenticity is the way power is exercised within it, our first question leads to another: *'What kind of community does the Church have to be?'*

Insofar as the Church can bring itself to walk in the light about the evils of abuse within it, it may be able to recover some sense of what it actually means to be the body of Christ, and to live that out in the real world, not the fantasy places of the stories we tell ourselves about ourselves. A church that manages to be half of what it claims to be would, indeed, be good news in a broken world.

This book is not an appeal to the Church to be nicer to people it has damaged, though that would be a start. More simple imagination, honesty, kindness, and compassion would be no bad thing. Nor do we want to suggest that the Church brings in an army of outside experts to clean up its mess and rescue it from the consequences of its bungling and dishonesty. Experts have a vital role in responding well to abuse, but their own particular contributions are not the same as the Church's core pastoral mission.

The Church of England needs to regain a humble confidence in its own calling, and to become what Leonard Sweet has hauntingly called:

> a Church with a big heart, dirty hands, and a beautiful mind. *(Tweet of 11.08.2018 at 0816)*

It may well feel deskilled for this by a tsunami of shame, and fear, arising from the sheer scale of its mistakes and dishonesty around safeguarding. Best leave the job to the experts.

That said, outside experts cannot help someone looking to detoxify their religion, to help them find hope again, a priest to pray for them, to offer spiritual counsel or anointing. It shocks some survivors when they are treated as simply social work cases, promised support that never materialises, in a way that devalues them and degrades the Church. All too often survivors have a queasy feeling they have found themselves in the self-service department of the Anglican Church where nobody ever offers to pray with or for anybody, compassion is strictly rationed, and resources are scant, in spite of the millions under the mattress.

This book is about attitudes more than procedures. We hope it will not harm, but heal the Church, helping it to rediscover its primary pastoral identity and task. This means, at the very least, acting as any member of the public would reasonably expect it to act when it has damaged people.

Culture change like this is hard work, time consuming and costly. But whenever the Church actually behaves like the Good Samaritan, rather than the priest or the Levite, it earns trust and respect. Only by doing this can it recover authenticity, confidence and credibility.

The Second Letter of Peter calls on persecuted Christians in Rome to resist narcissism and self-pity, reflect on the provisionality of everything in a fragile and perishing world, then ask what is in some ways the hardest question of all:

> Since all these things are to be dissolved in this way, what sort of persons ought you to be in leading lives of holiness and godliness? (II Peter 3:11)

The hardest of questions could be the most rewarding to answer properly.

We began with a poem by Lucy Berry, and end with another that challenges the Church to get real and, in the power of the Spirit, to confront its obsessions with status, control and face saving, for its own good, so as to advance the peace and salvation of all the world:

Empire and a Village

You and I, inside us, have an Empire and a village.
Admit it and acknowledge.
Now, let's forage for our courage.

Citizens of Empire are the haywire folk of hellfire;
of hiring, firing, miring, and of razor-wire and gunfire.

Citizens of Empire never listen to the village.
Empire will imprison any prophet of the village.

Empire has the cash, the whips, the slaves, and the advantage.
Empire screams for tribute which the village cannot manage.

Empire drinks the river and the village feels the shortage.
Empire starts the carnage and the village needs the bandage.

People of the village must rummage through the rubbish,
calling through the garbage for the children in the wreckage.

Empire knows to massage every message to the village;
to authorise as classified each image of the pillage.

Empire feeds off doubt and debt and luxury and slaughter.
Village dreams of crumbs of bread and never-ending water.

All of us, inside us, have an Empire and a village.
Admit it and acknowledge.
Now. Go forage for your courage.

© Lucy Berry 2018
(permission granted for non-profit reproduction)

Appendix 1
The Cast List

Names from our 15 Tales from the Crypt crop up at various points in our argument as examples. This simple handlist is designed to make it easier to relate the story to the character.

Alison 13
The vicar of St John's church who took Dan and Yvette's baby's funeral and subsequently found their planned memorial fell foul of the diocesan Chancellor's taste.

Alistair 15
A theological student at St Vincent's college, who sexually assaulted Lucy. A former international Hockey player, thrown off his course by the college authorities in response to her complaint.

Angela 5
Churchwarden at David and Karen's church, St Nat's. She has high ideals for faith and marriage, and is so shocked when she sees Karen's bruises that she promises secrecy rather than reporting the signs of abuse she has seen.

Anita 1
Wife of Mark. They met when she was one of his junior scout leaders at St Agatha's. She was less deeply committed to the church, not a server, but as a fellow introvert was happy to become more involved with the church through her young husband and his family.

Anna 2
Came from an unchurched background, but joined the church choir as a teenager with her friend Suzy. She was delighted and flattered by the attention of Vince, the charismatic young curate, but things did not end well.

Father Archie   1

The larger than life traditional Anglo-Catholic priest of St Agatha's church. A well-known community figure from the days he strode around the parish in his cassock during the Blitz, he came in 1937 and stayed for over forty years. He baptised Mark, whose mother Pauline became an active member of the church community through his kindness and encouragement.

Barry   6

Treasurer of Malcolm's urban middle-of-the-road Parish. He is prickly and people walk in some awe of him. There is a good personal reason for his manner, but this does not stop him being a difficult and fractious member of the PCC and local establishment, often experienced as a bully.

Bob   15

The senior student at St Gabriel's Theological College. He takes his role to heart, with a lively and well informed interest in the personal and pastoral circumstances of his fellow students, including Lucy.

Brian   14

The new vicar of St Peter's, where Norman, who is gay, has his roots. Brian went to visit Norman after his partner's death, and persuaded him back into the life of the church. He is a good-hearted and effective pastor, an Open Evangelical, who is careful not to let his personally affirmative convictions about gay people cause divisions at church. He knows things are changing, but for now is content to follow National Church Policy.

Chris   8

The archdeacon who receives and tries to help a churchwarden with her concerns about Jason's gross professional misconduct, using the Clergy Discipline Measure procedure.

Claire 12

The bishop's Chaplain who tried to help Jennifer. She was good pastorally, but could not do much to move things forward, or persuade the diocese to lift its £500 cap on payments towards counselling.

Craig 12

Jennifer's husband. It was the breakup of his marriage to Jennifer that triggered her disclosure of previous abuse in church.

Daniel 14

Norman's partner over many years. The relationship had led to Norman being thrown out of his parish church, and it was Daniel's funeral that brought Norman back into contact with the Church of England.

David Hamilton 5

Karen's husband. A Conservative Evangelical vicar, who met her at University, and to whom he had been married for 20 years at the time of her disclosure of his abuse.

Dan and Yvette 13

Parents of Baby Connor, who they brought to church to be christened, and who suffered a cot death. The local church responded to their need with compassion, but their tastes fell foul of that of the senior legal officer of the diocese.

Desmond 1

Dean of the Cathedral in the diocese where Mark was abused. His experience of dealing with abused people is not very consonant with the messages coming from the top, but it's worked for the senior staff of which he's been a part for many years.

Derek 14

Vicar of St Peter's. Derek's outlook on questions of human sexuality is entirely conventional for his generation, but he wants to be nice about it, of course.

Eileen   6

Married to Barry, the long-established treasurer of the church where Malcolm is vicar. Theirs has been a long partnership but very much on Barry's terms. During his funeral visit following Eileen's death, Malcolm learns why Barry behaves as he does.

Fiona   3

The long-standing Receptionist for the Holy Trinity Parish Office, and a co-worker with Jenny. A kind and resourceful friend who tries to care for Jenny, and to warn her about Mike.

Gemma   1

Journalist on the local paper who knows Mark from reporting his scouting activities, and writes up his story when he needs to go to the Press.

Geoff   7

Former Police Officer, who is ordained and becomes a curate. His broad and varied experience of life has not equipped him to meet the challenges of clergy culture within the Church.

Hayley   12

Jennifer's friend at work who helps and supports her when she discloses her abuse by a church organist.

Harriet   6

A younger member of Malcolm's PCC, with a few ideas of her own about how to bring the parish up to date. Trying to get things done in church as she would elsewhere brings her into conflict with Barry.

Helen   11

Jane's Ministry Development Reviewer. Every diocese has a scheme for Ministry Development Review, for which the bishop is responsible. These reviews are often largely carried out by others agreed on between the people concerned. They sometimes show up deeper problems than they were designed to help with, but are none the less useful for that.

Howard 13
Assistant Diocesan Registrar in the diocese where Alison is vicar, trying to minister to Dan and Yvette's following their baby's cot death. Diocesan Registrars are qualified solicitors who act as principal legal advisers to diocesan bishops, and in larger dioceses sometimes have assistants to deal with the volume of business.

Father Ian Montgomery 1
Vicar of St Agatha's, and Mark's abuser in the Vicarage when he was a boy server at the church.

Jane 11
Very conscientious vicar, devastated by a Clergy Discipline Measure complaint about her work from the hierarchy. It's hard to get away from a suspicion that the real issue is a service Jane put together with a gay couple that has been noticed from on high.

Janet 1
Bishop Simon's Chaplain, who helped the Church respond well to Mark's needs in the alternative ending to his story (Mark 2).

Jason 6
Vicar with Narcissistic Personality Disorder, who works out his own needs using the people he comes across in his parish.

Jennifer 12
Abused by a church organist as a girl, Jennifer discovers that there is a limit to the assistance the Church is willing to offer in her circumstances.

Jenny 3
Young Christian who leaves University and finds what she hopes will be her dream job as a Secretary to the vicar in a large town centre Evangelical church.

John 13
Curate to Alison, the vicar who ministers pastorally to Dan and Yvette following the death of their baby.

Jolyon 4

Victim of abuse at Public School Camps. His story on the news led to the camp leader being sentenced to eight years for child sex offences, and triggered Peter's memories.

Jonathan (Rufus) 10

New and dynamic vicar of St Joe's – he sets up a mentoring scheme and drafts Ryan into it against the better instincts of Ryan's partner Bethany. He picked up his moniker at Prep School and it stuck.

Jonty 9

Vicar of St Sam's. Damaged Boarding School survivor, with a special ministry towards younger people and a way of coming on strong when dealing with vulnerable older people.

Karen 5

Karen and David seemed to have the perfect Christian marriage, but it wasn't quite that. Karen felt unable to disclose her abuse because it would feel like a betrayal of what she believed.

Linda 8

Churchwarden at St Barnabas. Linda had the courage to bring a CDM against her vicar Jason who was frequently drunk, made lewd comments and bullied members of the congregation.

Lucinda 1

Communications Officer for Mark's diocese. Part of the team that worked on limiting the reputational damage of Mark's case.

Lucy 15

Ordinand Lucy was assaulted by another ordinand. The Principal of the college persuaded her not to go to the police. The Director of Ordinands betrayed the confidentiality that they had agreed.

Malcolm 6

Bullied vicar. Barry the treasurer bullied not only Malcolm but other members of the church and Malcolm felt unable to confront this.

The Cast List

Mark   1

Altar boy abused. Mark was abused by his vicar as a child and then re-abused by the failure of the Church to respond to his disclosure.

Martin   12

Samaritans Counsellor. Jennifer called them when she was feeling suicidal and she told him the story of her abuse by the organist at church.

Mike   3

Jenny's vicar at Holy Trinity. Within the church context his pattern of unwanted physical closeness was normalised and very difficult to challenge.

Moira   12

Jennifer's counsellor whose fees were not paid in full by the Church. This non-payment then left Jennifer in deeper debt.

Muriel   9

A woman who helps at the 8 o'clock communion service. A lay volunteer bullied by Jonty, a boarding school survivor.

Noreen   6

Church Secretary sacked by Barry while the vicar Malcom was on holiday. Malcom felt unable to face up to Barry and do the right thing.

Norman   15

Left the church due to homophobic behaviour. He returned after his partner died, but despite assurances experienced more abuse.

Patrick   1

Diocesan Secretary. Part of the senior team who worked together to limit the reputational damage to the Church in Mark's case thereby failing to meet his needs.

Peter 4
Barrister who attended a public school Evangelical boys' camp when young. He had not continued in the church after his early experiences, but an item on the TV news several years later raised disturbing memories for him.

Phil 14
Prayer Group leader at St Peter's church. Wanted to pray for Norman's 'same sex attraction' issues.

Father Robert 1
Mark's third parish priest. He did report what Mark had disclosed but was impotent in the face of the way the system handled Mark.

Roy 15
Lucy's Diocesan Director of Ordinands. He decided to deal with her disclosure in house and was not able to keep his promise of confidentiality.

Ryan and Bethany 10
Abused through Mentoring scheme. Through his use of theology and grooming, Ryan's vicar Rufus undermined their marriage.

Sally 7
Geoff's Training Incumbent. She chipped away at Geoff's self-confidence and used her power in inappropriate ways.

Sheila 1
Diocesan Safeguarding Adviser in Mark's diocese. She was not kept fully informed and was unaware of the way the original complaint had been swept under the carpet.

Stanley 1
Head Server at St Agatha's who trained many boys over the years, including Mark.

Steve 1
Archdeacon who offered £500 towards counselling for Mark, if

needed. Passed the pastoral responsibility to Father Robert who felt it was really a matter for Mark's spiritual director.

Tania 4

BBC Radio Journalist. She was investigating abuse at the Public School holiday camps Peter had attended. He knew interesting and pertinent information but was unable to go on record through fear or possible repercussions for his career.

Tony and Dave 11

Gay couple for whom Jane, their vicar, devised a service of thanksgiving and dedication that seems to have rubbed the powers that be up the wrong way.

Veronica 13

Diocesan Chancellor. Senior legal authority in the Consistory Court of the diocese. According to her registrar, her graveyard rules were devised according to her personal taste.

Vince 2

Abusive priest with Anna, very skilled at grooming. Played on teenage need to feel special.

Appendix 2
Key to Stories

Name	Circs	Metier	Sex	Abuse Types	Model
1. Mark	Altar boy abused	A/Cath	M	Sx Sp	CH VS PH PF
2. Anna	Pregnant Teenager	C/Lib	F	Sp	VS CH
3. Jenny	Office worker	Op. Ev.	F	B Sx Sp	CH VS
4. Peter	Barrister on Camp	C. Ev	M	Ps Sp B	MC VS CH
5. Karen	Domestic Violence	C. Ev	F	Ps Ph Em Sp Sx	BVS MC
6. Malcolm	Bullied Vicar	C/Lib	M	Ps E B	MC HS
7. Geoff	Bullied Curate	C/Lib	M	Ps B	MC PH PF
8. Jason	Psychopathic	Ch. Ev	F	Sp B	CH VS MC HS DT
9. Muriel	Bullied volunteer	Ch. Ev.	F	B PF Sp	MC CH PH PF
10. Ryan & Bethany	Grooming /SA	Ch. Ev.	M/F	Ps Em Sp	DT VS MC
11. Jane	CDM Victim	C/Lib	F	Ps Sp B	MC DT HS
12. Jennifer	Limited help	C/Lib	F	Sx F Sp B	VS CH PF
13. Dan & Yvette	Baby memorial	C/Lib	M/F	E B	VS CH PF
14. Norman	Gay church returner	Op. Ev.	M	Ps E Sp	CH VS MC
15. Lucy	Ordinand assault	A/Cath	F	Ps Sp B Sx	VS MC HS

Church style
A/Cath (Anglo Catholic) C/Lib (Central / Liberal) C.Ev (Conservative Evangelical) Ch.Ev (Charismatic Evangelical) Op.Ev (Open Evangelical)
Abuse Types
Bullying, Emotional, Financial, Psychological, **Physical**, **Sexual**, **Spiritual**
Models
Hot Stove (**HS**), Swiss Cheese (**CH**), TA (**DT**), Vector/Signature (**VS**), Mind Control (**MC**) Woes of Pharisees (**PH**) Pope Francis List (**PF**)

Appendix 3
Duluth Power Wheel

All abuse involves power. The Duluth Model was developed from the work of Ellen Pence and Michael Paymar at the Domestic Abuse Intervention Project in Duluth MN. The Power Wheel is its diagnostic tool. It does not include spiritual abuse, and may be thought by some to be stereotypically gendered, but it may indicate some warning lights to help identify the 'Coercive Control' that English Law now recognises as a crime.

www.theduluthmodel.org

215

Appendix 4
Bad Lasagne

A big Gospel principle is to 'do to others as you would have them do to you.'

Unfortunately senior Church officials, especially those at the top of a deferential culture, often experience very different day-to-day lives from the victims of abuse. The imaginative leap necessary to see things from the other side of the room in the midst of a busy day can be a considerable challenge.

This simple test is designed to engage empathy about things that could be heard on such occasions. It may help those in high office to use their imaginations more fruitfully by applying them to something very much simpler that should be more commonplace than spiritual abuse.

What is heard is not the same thing as what was said, let alone what was intended. There is no suggestion any food shop would dream of saying any of these things. But what if they were heard to have said them? The way to use this 'Bad Lasagne' Guide is to ask, for each possible response, 'How would I feel if a senior manager said that to me?'

You have bought a lasagne from a well-known high street supermarket with pretensions and something of a reputation for fine food. Unfortunately it has made you very ill. You contact the shop concerned and, after some difficulty finding out whom to complain to and how, the person from the shop says:

- We are a leading food producer in the UK and it could not have been our lasagne
- You will be hearing from us (but you don't)
- You must have had a dirty plate
- You must have cooked it badly, so it's all your fault really

- We can give you £500, but only if you promise not to tell anyone our lasagne made you ill
- We are really sorry this has happened to you, and we will look into it – then silence
- You are very sick – we cannot be expected to deal rationally with very sick people
- We did not intend you to be ill, so it can't be our fault
- If you had never eaten it you would not have been ill – you decided to eat it so you must share the responsibility with us
- If the store hadn't sold it to you, you'd be OK. So it's all the fault of the checkout assistant who served you. We can't take any responsibility beyond that.
- Have another one?
- You can't expect things to be perfect all the time. We're all imperfect people. You're too pushy...
- The sickness didn't actually happen in our shop so we can't be absolutely sure it's our fault
- We produce healthy delicious food. How dare you think it's our fault. You'll be hearing from our solicitors if you say we made you ill.
- Forgiveness is a very noble thing. Why can't you just forgive and move on?
- We have good procedures in place now to prevent this happening again. Why rake up the past?
- You are obviously in league with our competitors
- Why are you doing this to us?
- It's a free country. If you don't want to buy our lasagne, there are plenty of other shops out there.

If any of these words and phrases strikes you as problematic if you had been heard to say them by the other person (whatever you intended), please find something else to say.

Unfortunately the food poisoning turns out to be E.coli. How would you have reacted on behalf of the shop if your sick complainant's E.coli had caused something life changing, say

long term renal failure leading to a long time off work, a lost job, or long-term disability?

The principle is simple. In 1982 a murderer injected poison into containers of Tylenol, a leading US analgesic. Its manufacturers, Johnson & Johnson, found themselves plunged into a serious practical and reputational crisis. The company's response, generally taken as a textbook example of good practice, involved immediate product recall, and, eventually, a successful relaunch of the product. At its heart, however, was the Chief Executive, basing his words on the company's 'Credo', its statement of values, taking full and personal responsibility for what had happened, even though, of course, the company bore no direct responsibility for the murderer's actions.

Handwringing protestations that the Church is complicated and bishops are only bishops and can't be held responsible or actually do anything without their lawyers' permission seem to survivors of abuse in Church to be lame, to put it mildly.

Abusing the Bible

The misuse of holy text is a powerful part of spiritual abuse. In the stories survivors tell, especially after domestic abuse of the sort endured by Karen (5), a few texts crop up again and again.

Matthew 18: 15

If another member of the church sins against you, go and point out the fault when the two of you are alone.

Jesus lays down a principle that believers should sort out their differences between themselves. This principle is admirable for regular fallings out between disciples, but needs very careful handling when we apply it to abusive behaviour. Any suggestion that an abusee should have to sort matters out in the first instance with their abuser is, in itself, inherently abusive.

Jason (8) has been drunk and spiritually domineering. When victims try to take disciplinary action against him, he uses Matthew 18 against them. He tells the bishop 'the Bible says if they've got a complaint about me, they should come and discuss it with me first. It's the Christian way.'

It is unreasonable to require people he has been bullying to negotiate with him one by one and in person. Any process that leaves power in the hands of a possible abuser compounds abuse. Practically speaking, the power balance in Jason's relationship with his parishioners is so unequal it is simply not credible to think this could be a viable way forward.

Matthew 6:14-15

> For if you forgive others their trespasses, your heavenly
> Father will also forgive you; but if you do not forgive others,
> neither will your Father forgive your trespasses.

Jesus demands unconditional forgiveness. This noble aspiration
can easily be turned against abuse victims. It is simply wrong for
an abuser or Church official to try and guilt-trip someone into
saying they forgive. Compelling anyone to forgive before they are
ready to do so is cruel and unrealistic. It cannot possibly produce
healthy closure.

A particularly bizarre example of forgiveness ideals being
misapplied was recorded by IICSA in 2018. A former Dean of
Chichester Cathedral piled the files of abusing clergy onto a
bonfire because he seems to have considered that since God had
forgiven them there was no longer any reason to keep a record of
what they had done.

Ephesians 5:22-4

> Wives, be subject to your husbands as you are to the Lord.
> For the husband is the head of the wife just as Christ is the
> head of the church, the body of which he is the Saviour. Just
> as the church is subject to Christ, so also wives ought to be,
> in everything, to their husbands.

Karen's abusive husband David (5) used this text as a charter for
his domestic abuse.

The question at issue is how power is used in the relationship.
When St Paul says 'the husband is the head of the wife as Christ
is the head of the Church, his body' is this 'head' a co-dependent
organ, or a controlling oppressor? Any man who cannot imagine
the Lord Jesus as anything other than a domineering alpha male
like themselves is seriously misreading the way Jesus treated
women.

Genesis 2:18

The Lord said, it is not good for the man to be alone. I will make a helper suitable for him.

This text at the beginning of the Bible is also open to misogynistic use. You could read it as a charter for equality. The Puritan commentator Matthew Henry (1662-1714) suggested:

the woman was made of a rib out of the side of Adam; not made out of his head to rule over him, nor out of his feet to be trampled upon by him, but out of his side to be equal with him, under his arm to be protected, and near his heart to be beloved.

A more unreconstructed reading would say that women were created to be men's little helpers, like Father Christmas's elves – right up there with Santa ringing their bells, of course, but never driving the sleigh.

Genesis 3:6

When the woman saw that the fruit of the tree was good for food and pleasing to the eye, and also desirable for gaining wisdom, she took some and ate it. She also gave some to her husband who was with her and he ate it.

A more totalising and pervasive root of Christian misogyny has been the story of the Fall. The whole human race fell from paradise, and it was all Eve's fault. Nothing any daughter of Eve can say or do can ever change that fact.

Adam was not deceived, but the woman was deceived and became a transgressor. (1 Timothy 2:14)

The next verse holds out a bleak hope:

Yet she will be saved through childbearing, provided she continues in faith and love and holiness, with modesty.

One could say, however, though few seem to, that whilst Eve disobeyed God Adam hadn't the gumption to disobey her. The moral of the tale becomes 'independent thought and equal negotiation is a better idea than gender stereotypical roleplay.'

1 Peter 1:6

> In all this you greatly rejoice though now for a little while you may have to suffer grief in all kinds of trials.

Christians can have strange fixations about suffering. Some have pictured it as something of a virtue in itself. This carries a risk that people who complain about being hurt will simply be told their suffering is necessary or even in some way redemptive. David (5) used this verse as ammunition in his row with Karen. David needs to know that all suffering is not good in itself. The pain of which the text speaks was probably persecution by the Emperor Nero. Why should any Christian think it is virtuous to persecute another, least of all one they are married to? And why would any Christian who knew what was going on side with the persecutor, not their victim?

Matthew 5:32

> I tell you anyone who divorces his wife except for sexual immorality makes her the victim of adultery.

Appeals to a dogma about Christian marriage and family life are particularly bizarre. In the face of received family practice, Jesus applied words about a man divorcing his wife to a wife divorcing her husband. Any attitude to the family that makes it into a sacred cow is entirely different from that of Jesus Christ in the Gospels. He treated claims of clan and family allegiance very lightly –

> Another said, 'I will follow you, Lord; but let me first say farewell to those at my home.' Jesus said to him, 'No one

who puts a hand to the plow and looks back is fit for the kingdom of God.' (Luke 9:61)

While he was still speaking to the crowds, his mother and his brothers were standing outside, wanting to speak to him. Someone told him, 'Look, your mother and your brothers are standing outside, wanting to speak to you.' But to the one who had told him this, Jesus replied, 'Who is my mother, and who are my brothers?' And pointing to his disciples, he said, 'Here are my mother and my brothers! For whoever does the will of my Father in heaven is my brother and sister and mother.' (Matthew 12:46-50)

It is hard to disagree with Don Cupitt's puzzlement about the twentieth-century Church's idolisation of the nuclear family:

It appears from the gospels that Jesus was highly critical of the family for strong religious reasons. For him, the call of the Kingdom was away from family roles, not into them. The idealisation of the family is a modern cultural creation, which the churches have validated and now no modern bishop would dream of publicly endorsing Jesus' views about the family.